D1605767

The Influences of
RUDOLPH LABAN

The Influences of
RUDOLPH LABAN

John Foster, MA, MEd

Principal, Lady Mabel College of Education
Wentworth, Rotherham, S. Yorks.

LEPUS BOOKS • LONDON

ISBN 0 86019 015 3

Typesetting by Malvern Typesetting Services
Printed in Great Britain at the
University Printing House, Cambridge

CONTENTS

CONTENTS

Section C: Higher Education

PREFACE

This book has been developed from a post-graduate research scheme carried out under the guidance of Professor W. H. G. Armytage at the University of Sheffield, to whom I record my thanks for his help and guidance.

My thanks are also due to colleagues and students at Lady Mabel College who have been generous with their time in assisting me.

The book could not have been produced without the help of many physical educationists who were interviewed as part of the original research. Many of these people are named in the text but I would like to record my thanks to all who helped in this way.

The aim has been to examine and evaluate the influence of Rduolph Laban on English Education. It was never the intention to write a biography and bibliographical material has only been included if it had not been previously published or if it shed particular light on the thesis.

Much of the material concerning Laban is 'Arts' orientated. It is concerned with Dance as an art form, and is not focused towards the educational uses of Laban's ideas. This has meant that much published material was irrelevant to this brief. As a result of this, however, few answers have emerged. Rather, questions have been raised, areas of dispute identified and growth points designated.

PART ONE
LABAN – THE MAN

The early years

Even Laban's name is open to question. He is referred to by Thornton (1971) as Varalja vereknye esliger faly Laban Rezso Keresztelo Szent Janos Attila and as Rudolph Jean-Marie Laban by Brown and Sommer (1969). The Laban Art of Movement Guild, in a special birthday number published in their magazine in December 1954, addresses him deferentially in the text as Mr Laban, while contributors to this issue acknowledge his charismatic aura by referring to him simply as Laban. Though many of these contributors were his contemporaries and colleagues none refers to him by his christian name. Oscar Bienz, an old pupil who knew Laban before 1916, refers to him as Rudolph von Laban, Laban de Laban; and later, in another letter, as Count Laban. Typical of the reactions of those who knew him is summed up in the phrase 'he was the master'.

Laban was born in Bratislava in 1879. He was the son of an army general and travelled widely as a boy as his father moved from posting to posting. It is possible to show that some of his later ideas are rooted in this period of his early life. In answering the question, 'What has led you to study movement?' Laban (1951) admits the influence of Dervish rituals and the dogma of Balkan monastic institutions. He writes:

> I got access to these rituals through a temporary tutor of mine, an Imam (Mohamedan priest). He was the only learned man on a vast high plateau in the mountains where my father was stationed. My talks with this man belong to the unforgettable treasures of my mind. We talked about the wisdom, the dignity and happiness of man and he told and showed me a lot about the dancing and the exercises in religious rituals.

In an earlier article, he talks about the influence of eastern dance, Greek drama (old and new), and the rituals of Red Indians. Also, he was loud in his praise of the Chinese theatre which he called, 'the highest cultivated stage dancing in the world' (Laban 1947). There is some doubt about whether he actually visited China although his publishers claim that he did (See Laban 1966).

Oscar Bienz, a former student, has reported on Laban's early life and detailed his contacts with Austrian court circles. Bienz was informed by Laban that the latter's father was War Minister at the Austrian Court of Emperor Franz-Joseph. There is no doubt that during his early years he did travel widely and that these journeys provided him with experiences which affected his later thinking. Laban studied in Paris from 1900 to 1907 and pursued various courses at the École des Beaux Arts. He refers to 'pictures and drawings of my first "Saltarium", a building which I devised during my study of architecture at the École des Beaux Arts in Paris around 1900'.

Lisa Ullmann states that:

> Laban never did any drawings for a proposed Saltarium. He designed on several occasions a dance theatre.

Such a drawing is reproduced in his autobiography (Laban 1935). Laban's study in Paris is open to controversy. Leeder doubted whether Laban studied in Paris to any great extent. He thought he may have been attracted by the people concerned with the Arts who were working there at the time, but his view was that the idea of sustained study there by Laban was a myth which Laban had allowed to grow, and done something to foster. Leeder saw a side of his personality which enjoyed a practical joke and he felt that Laban may have built up his Parisian experiences originally out of a sense of fun. This sense of humour is also commented upon by several contributors to the *Laban Guild Magazine Birthday Number* (December 1954).

It is difficult to be exact about this period in Laban's life. No one who is alive can authenticate his activities at this time and there are no records. Laban (1947) recalls:

> My so-called 'Archives' were twice destroyed in the two world wars. Not a scrap of paper, not even one piece of other valuable

collections of things referring to my movement research has been left over. All burned, bombed, blown into the air.

Indeed, Laban's recollections and personal interpretations of his early life are considered by Curl (1967a) to be extremely suspect. After an extensive study of his autobiography (Ein Leben fur den Tanz) he found it:

> difficult to distinguish between actual and imagined events, for he plays so freely across the line of fantasy and fact. Inner and outer worlds become fused in a mythical play of demons, spirits and everyday folk.

A study of Lisa Ullmann's translation of this work supports this view. Ullmann's annotations certainly help to distinguish between 'fantasy and fact' but one cannot help but be aware of Laban's indulgent style and his reticence to treat his material logically.

There is little in the Laban archives to help the researcher elucidate much about his early life. Indeed there is little there concerned with Movement and Education which has not been published in the Laban Art of Movement Guild magazine. The archives are housed in one cupboard. It is reasonable to assume that in the seventeen years since his death, any material not published whilst he was alive would have been published since that time in the magazine devoted to spreading his ideas. The Laban archives as the source of untold truths is a myth. It is a fantasy idea perpetrated often in the Guild magazine and by some of the people close to Laban in his last years. To comment on the archives, there is little here attributable to Laban before 1938. Many of the documents have the stamp of being prepared in a hurry, often as scribbled notes, just prior to his death. At this time, he probably felt that much of his early thinking and ideas had not been documented. This work is often the recollection of thoughts, ideas, innovations and presentations of his life before 1938. This is consistent with the fact that his previous 'archives' had been lost and destroyed. He would feel the need to commit himself to paper once more as he realized that his life was drawing to a close. The disorganized nature of the archives is illustrated by the fact that the Laban Guild magazine once published an article which it attributed to Laban which was subsequently found to be his notes on the work of another author! (A situation which was remedied by an apology in a subsequent issue of the magazine.)

In the years before World War I, Laban organized dance festivals on the shores of Lake Maggiore, and was a member of an art colony there. This group gave theatrical performances, and also worked in an individual, creative manner which Laban was able to develop over the ensuing years. Local villagers watched and stayed to take part actively in the sessions. Here he worked with unsophisticated, simple country people with no knowledge of his style of dancing. It is possible that his first teaching styles may have been developed at this time. Certainly his dance notation was. He writes of 'my still fragmentary dance notation', and bemoans the fact that at the time, his notes were all lost. This lack of order and systematization are typical of Laban, and the researcher is poorer for this. Paradoxically, however, these same qualities may have been required to produce the creative ideas from which his main principles developed.

Switzerland provided him with plenty of scope. Bienz was Laban's pupil in 1916 in Zurich. He writes:

> Laban came in 1916 to Zurich and started a eurhythmic and personality cult which had great success, due to excellent propaganda, and the absence of any other ballet school. I was the first scholar.

He had very close associations with Laban at this time and was able to write authoritatively about Laban and in particular about his masonic connections. The texts of his letters are relevant, but are wide-ranging. Consequently they are only related in parts to each topic as it is presented. They are included, therefore, as appendix one. Relevant sections are used in the text as appropriate.

When he was in Switzerland, Laban was concerned with quasi-masonic activities (by today's masonic standards). Bienz reports, 'In my opinion, he was a shadow Cagliostro.' This means that he was a kind of wizard, using masonic ritual, and formulating ceremonies which tried to explain spiritual philosophies and ideas of immortality. Laban does not emerge from this period with much personal credit. Bienz again writes:

Trouble now or even before 1919 started in the Lodge on account of the speedy raising of Laban into higher degrees. Laban was advised to go to Germany apparently on account of his numerous alliances with women. He left leaving a lot of debts, 60,000 Swiss francs to the Worshipful Master and 5,000 borrowed from me and many others I know of which were never repaid.

Laban adopted a cavalier attitude to the values which were current in society at the time. Bienz provided a 'free translation' from a book by Carl Riess titled, *Ascona*, published in Switzerland in 1964, concerned with masonic history and the Arts Colony functioning in Ascona at the time. From page 80, concerning activities in 1919 it reads:

> Now a new man came, Theodore Reuss, who implied that he was a friend of Rudolph Steiner. Reuss stayed in England before the 1914-18 war. He pretended to have been a Grandmaster of several freemason's lodges. He proposed to Mr Oedenhoven, proprietor of the Monte Veritas (Ascona) lodge that Monte Veritas should be made the seat of a mystic Grand order.
>
> He found a lot of simple men who contributed large sums of money to this new venture, but no-one could make out what the order was about as only after 94 degrees were certain revelations made. Most of the bretheren did not go beyond the sixth degree except Laban.
>
> The whole business was a dreadful swindle. In 1917, Laban, von Varaga and Mary Wigman joined in but one day a leakage occurred proving that Reuss was an imposter. He was then excluded from the lodge.

Laban refers to his use of 'a former vegetarian colony' in his autobiography. Lisa Ullmann identifies this as Monte Veritas, Ticino, which was a centre for those interested in new approaches to the Arts. Laban was also active in a lodge called 'Verita Mystico'. This lodge grew out of the ideas of Reuss and was concerned with mysticism and esoteric teachings, ideas which permeated Laban's later thinking. Many of Laban's female students were initiated into this lodge. Hence these activities must be regarded as quasi-masonic as women are banned completely from masonic working under the United Grand Lodge in England.

Freemasonry in Switzerland 1910-1920 was poorly formulated with regard to set ritual. Much of the working was co-masonic and explored similar ideas to those of the theosophists in England, led by Annie Besant. The movement did attract free-thinkers and creative liberals searching for basic truths. Many active masons were exiles and there was a large Jewish element. However, Bienz reports that the introduction and initiation of women and subsequent immoral behaviour precluded real masonic science and the order fell into disrepute. It regained its stature as 'more conservative Swiss' became involved who re-established traditional masonic working and used the Scottish and English constitution.

The use which Laban made of masonic ideas is developed in part two when ideological debts are studied.

The period in Switzerland provided Laban with plenty of opportunities to develop his emerging interests. The accent was on consolidation of his earlier experiences, and an ordering of his ideas. The creative process has been described by Torrance (1962) in terms of the stages of preparation, incubation, illumination, and verification. After early preparation, the latent ideas for Laban's life's work were now beginning to take shape, and become illuminated in conscious thought. Movement choirs, notation, choreology (research into the art of movement), teaching styles, and ideas concerning space patterns and harmonies all had their genesis during this period, and were available to him for wider development over the years to come.

Laban was a prominent figure in the arts in Switzerland during the period 1910-20. His aimiability and presence contributed to his appeal. In the words of Bienz:

> He used his personal charm and magic to impress his personality cult on his dancers. He also made effective use of his high stature, over six feet tall.

It is his involvement with Dada-ism, however, which illustrates the real importance of Laban in the arts at this time.

The Dada movement was 'an artistic revolt against art' whose members had a reputation for rowdiness and questioning current values. 'Where next?' was their watchword. They could be compared to present-day hippies, yippies, drop-outs, alternative society advocates, and underground newspaper groups (Willett, 1970). 'Dada' quickly became a myth because of its notorious unconventionality at a time when the flouting of social custom was unusual.

The movement began in Switzerland about 1915-16. An article in the *Times Educational Supplement* on 23 October 1953 made the point that:

> The fact that Dada began life in Zurich and not in New York or Paris is significant, for the movement owes many of its characteristics to the peculiar atmosphere prevailing in that city at that time.

This is a reference to neutral Switzerland which at the time housed individuals from a range of the arts and politics who had found sanctuary there, but were still practising their somewhat avant-garde ideas.

Laban was closely connected with Dada. Richter (1965) gives many detailed accounts of his association and records in his diary for 2 April 1916:

> Leonard Frank and his wife visited the club. Also Herr von Laban with his Ladies (the dancers of the Laban schools).

He also quotes from Hugo Ball, 'a thinker and poet, philosopher, novelist, cabaret performer, journalist and mystic'. In the latter's diary, he notes:

> In the audience I saw Brupacher, Jelmoli, Laban and Frau Wigman. Fearing a debacle I pulled myself together.

Even here, Laban's presence was important!

Laban was obviously an influential member of the group, having under his tutelage the most eligible young ladies. Richter (1965) again reports:

> Sophie (Taeuber) was studying dancing under Laban in whose hallowed halls I was a frequent visitor . . . and the stern Laban might be concealing himself anywhere.

Was his interest proprietary, personal, professional or pastoral?

Leeder talked at interview about Laban and the Dada-ists. His comments generally support the picture given above. He talked of Laban developing his own dance form at the time. He originated solo-dances based mainly on hand movements where he wove patterns in space in a series of symbolic gestures. Leeder was unimpressed by these when he saw them later. He dismissed Laban in this guise as 'Harlequin in uniform', and saw him as a figure of fun. This was not Laban the grand innovator but a man in search of a new art form and seeking new media for expression. Of this work, Hugo Ball asked, 'Is sign-language the true language of paradise?' If we assume from this that he was impressed, it was probably because he had evolved an abstract phonetic poem as a new art-form and saw similarity of approach and a complementary creative process at work in both endeavours. His comment could be interpreted quite differently. Does he ask,

> Are we to believe that the most sublime expression of man's spiritual and rational being is to be found in the posturing of his physical body rather than through other expressions?

In view of Leeder's scathing comment, this may have been Ball's intention. The issue must be conjectural and remain a matter for opinion.

Laban's influence on the movement was considerable. Richter (1965) enlarges on Dada activities:

> If the Odeon was our terrestrial base, our celestial headquarters was Laban's ballet school. There we met young dancers of our generation. Mary Wigman, Maria Vanselow, Sophie Taeuber, Suzanne Perrotet, Maja Kruseck, Kathe Wulff and others. Only at fixed times were we allowed into this nunnery, with which we had more or less emotional ties, whether fleeting or permanent. These highly personal contacts – and Laban's revolutionary contribution to choreography – finally involved the whole Laban school in the Dada movement. Its students danced in the ballet Die Kaufleute. In front of abstract backdrops by Arp and myself, dancers wearing Janco's abstract masks fluttered like butterflies of Euson, drilled and directed according to a choreography written down by Kathe Wulff and Sophie Taeuber in Laban's system of notation.

Hans Ritchter is an eminent art historian and himself a considerable artist. He details the emotional involvements and attachments of a variety of people with Laban's pupils:

Into this rich field of perils we hurled ourselves as en-
thusiastically as we hurled ourselves into Dada. The two
things went together.

The influence of Dada on Laban is shown in the passage:

Dance as practised by the Dadaists as well as its particular kind
of incidental music has probably exerted some influence on
Rudolph von Laban and Mary Wigman who are both
mentioned as having been among the visitors of the Cabaret
Voltaire (Verkauf 1957).

This cabaret attracted some of the most eminent people of the
century. The circle in which Laban moved at that time can be
judged from the following statement:

In that thick smoke of the Cabaret Voltaire some sudden
apparition would loom up every now and then, like the
impressive Mongol features of Lenin, or Laban, the great
dancer, with his Assyrian beard.

Verkauf also links painters like Modigliani, Picasso,
Kandinsky, Leger and Matisse with the Dada group. It seems
impossible for Laban to have mixed in company like this
without being influenced by the ideas with which they were
concerned. Similarly, as a respected member of that group,
one understands that he influenced the others.

So close was Laban's association with Dada that his pupils
were performing in several scenes at the famous soirée in
Zurich on 9 April 1919 which erupted into an uncontrollable
riot. The involvement in Dadaism shows Laban's experimentation with multi-media, inter-disciplinary artistic
ventures. These interests were often reflected in his later work
in Education in England.

Laban's Dada-period provides us with a microcosm of the
life he led, his contacts, the innovative and research nature of
his work, the times and the man, and his search for a satisfying
art-form. Many of his ideas took shape at this time – the use
which would be made of them in thirty years' time would be
totally unforseeable during their inception.

Laban's romantic attachments reveal an intertwining of his
personal and professional interests. His numerous associations
with women who had connection with the theatre and dance

are known. Leeder described Laban as a 'womanizer'. He had 'a magnetic attraction for women. No-one was safe with him.' He spoke of a romantic involvement with Gertrude Loesser which gave him a great deal of satisfaction. Bienz supports the views expressed by Leeder. Referring to Laban's relationship with women, he writes:

> He cohabited with almost all the not-so-young dancers of his school, most of whom were Jewish.

Laban's women were drawn from the ranks of his pupils and fellow artists. His romances with Suzanne Perrotet and Dussia Bereska, both brilliant exponents of the new dance techniques, were referred to by many interviewees. Both bore a child by him. His first wife, Martha, a painter died about 1907. His second marriage in 1910, from which it appears there were five children, broke up in 1919. This wife, Maja (Maria Lederer), a concert singer, was still alive in 1973 aged about 88 years, and living in Munich. Laban was atypical as a father, having little close contact with his children. In this he can be compared with Rousseau. Lisa Ullmann rationalizes this behaviour in the phrase 'All his pupils were his children.' Little is known of his relationship with Lisa Ullmann except that she was his close colleague and confidante from 1938 until his death twenty years later. As with his other associates, she was connected with his work and interests and influenced him greatly. The application of his ideas to English Education can be attributed to her in a large measure (see part three). Leonard Elmhirst, the founder of Dartington Hall knew Laban well. He writes:

> Lisa took infinite pains to look after Laban's interest and ideas and welfare and served him devotedly to the end. In the process she certainly kept at arm's length any woman whom she thought might catch his eye and regarded those who did with a certain feline antagonism.

Laban's romantic attachments are in the tradition of the Behemian set of the early years of this century. His contact with the arts and artists in many disciplines in Paris, his connections with the Dada art movement, his dance schools and his own magnetic personality took him outside traditional marital relationships. These attachments, often with gifted artists, reflect his interests and the way of life which was his before he came to England. There is a dichotomy between this image, and the one portrayed in the last years of his life, and since, by his English colleagues, who came from a more traditional, English, middle-class, teaching background.

In Germany after World War I

Laban returned to Germany after World War I and established himself as a leading figure in the dance world. His first school in Stuttgart attracted many pupils who were to find fame subsequently in their own right. Other schools followed and soon Laban enjoyed a national reputation.

At this time, he was able to demonstrate the validity of his movement principles in a variety of media. Exploration of his ideas was carried out at dance schools which he established all over Germany, and in Switzerland, Budapest, Zagreb, Rome, Vienna and Paris. They experimented with dance and movement on a theatrical, therapeutic, remedial, educational and purely intrinsically pleasurable basis. Laban himself was busy as a choreographer, writer, producer and festival director. In the latter category, he visited factories and workshops and became interested in 'working movement and the psychological attitudes of industrial man.' He functioned here as a movement consultant, a role he was to adopt again in England during World War II. Indeed, it was at this time that Laban can be shown to be a visionary, an innovator and precursor of present-day time and motion, and organization and method study. He employed observational study techniques to improve work-rates and conditions in the early 1920s which are still common today. Indeed, his collaboration with F. C. Lawrence in England during the 1939-1945 war was a direct extension of this early work in Germany, and led to the publication of *Effort* (Laban & Lawrence, 1947) shortly afterwards.

In the 1920s in Germany, there were many great artists and innovators at work whose lives touched Laban and his work.

In his own discipline Kurt Jooss and Mary Wigman were two of Laban's most famous pupils who both found fame in their own right. Influences between them all were reciprocal. Both Jooss and Wigman developed work from Laban and in many senses grew away from him but they formed a sounding platform for ideas they shared. Leeder and Knust, at interview, testified to these views and laid emphasis on the hospitality afforded to Laban by Jooss on his arrival in England in 1938. They stressed the importance to Laban of having Jooss here as a friend and helper and the value of the security which Jooss represented.

The closeness of the Laban/Jooss association is seen by Mayerova (1957). She says:

> And yet in 1922, after the victory of 'The Green Table' in Paris, we all believed that a turning point had been reached. Even so I consider that the date of 'The Green Table' marks the beginning of a new era for the dancer, for it was the first indisputable display of a new Art of the Dance based on the revolutionary theories of Laban.

Even at this time, the two men were working together and their work was complementary – each supported the other.

Mary Wigman was something more than Laban's pupil:

> She (Wigman) studied with the innovator Rudolph von Laban but surpassed him and all her colleagues in achievement. She discovered new ways of moving, the ebb and flow of motion, the expansion of power and its release (De Mille, 1963; Hall, F., 1953).

The feedback from Wigman's imaginative development of his work set Laban re-appraising his ideas. In this sphere:

> Wigman placed her dance consciously in a three dimensional area, relating the moving figure always to its surroundings in what might be called an architectural sense. Laban's experiments with space had been largely intellectual; he had seen the human body as standing theoretically in the centre of a many sided geometric figure, and had formulated the directions and the extents and the paths of travel in which its various members could move. Wigman developed this emotionally – she felt space as the medium through which she moved in much the same way as the swimmer feels the water – her movement was conceived in the inner processes of her individual psychology (Martin, 1946).

Prunella Stack saw Wigman perform in 1936 and comments in her autobiography, on the highly dramatic and emotional

quality of her performance and the feverish reception
accorded to it by the German audience. She found this to be
a paradox when compared to the rigid discipline and
regimentation existing in Germany at that time. Pressure must
have been evident then, however, as Wigman left Germany
shortly afterwards.

In a related discipline, the work of Carl Orff is relevant.
Although several writers have suggested personal contact
between Orff and Laban, the former himself practically denies
this. Through Margaret Murray, his English agent and friend,
Orff writes that he never 'came to know' Laban but they did
communicate by letter. Laban was present at the first
performance of Carmina Burana. He should have choreo-
graphed this but did not do so for some unknown reason.
Afterwards he wrote to Orff in 'charming and appreciative terms' about the performance.

In a similar view, Orff (1964) speaking in England puts
Laban and himself in the same cadre. Today we would regard
them as participants in the same 'think-tank':

> To return to how it all began; it was in the twenties. A new
> feeling for physical activity, for the practice of sport, gymnastics
> and dancing had seized the youth of Europe. The work and
> ideas of Jacques-Dalcroze that had spread all over the world
> helped considerably to prepare the ground for a new interest in
> physical education. Laban and Wigman, to mention only two
> names, *were near to the zenith of their careers*. Rudolph von
> Laban was without doubt one of the most important dance
> teachers and choreographers of his time and his writings about
> dance made him internationally famous. The highly gifted
> Mary Wigman created a new kind of expressive dancing. The
> work of both these had considerable influence in artistic and
> educational circles and it was at this time in Germany that many
> gymnastic and dance schools were founded. All these enterprises
> were of great interest to me, for they were all closely connected
> with my work.

The Orff/Laban influences were again two-way. Orff's early
work was very much music/movement integrated. Showing
how music and movement were incorporated together he says:

> For the first time (when schools broadcasts were undertaken),

Schulwerk could be taught in the fullness as we had always visualized it (Orff, 1964).

In a speech made in 1964, Orff linked his work with that of Laban. This link has been cemented more recently:

It is this spontaneity and wholeness which both Laban and Orff, through the application of their ideas, aimed to preserve and to re-awaken and retain into adult life (Morley 1972).

Kurt Hahn was another figure in the same strain as many already mentioned. He was in many ways the complete antithesis of Laban. But then, by Laban's own principles, such people may be drawn together. J. M. Hogan, who was concerned with Hahn in the setting up of the first outward-bound school at Aberdovey, said that when they met, Laban and Hahn emphasized their differences but always recognized a common core between them. They were both concerned to achieve Sir Robert Birley's 'personal responsibility' in their pupils but by different means. Hahn (1970) was aware of the need:

to encourage boys to develop as responsible individuals, strong in mind and character to reject the standards of the mob, and to resist the temptation to run with the herd.

Laban believed that movement aids the understanding of one's own behaviour and furthers the enrichment of individual response and personality integration (Redfern 1973). The views of both Hahn and Laban have common endpoints. Hogan rightly emphasizes their differences but it is a mark of the men's flexibility that they could learn from each other about process. They were also aware of fundamentally similar goals in their work.

The work of Rudolph Steiner must be mentioned if one examines the ideas which are contained in Laban's books published in Germany in the 1920s. Sometimes referred to as an anthroposophist, but mainly regarded as a social philosopher and educationist, Steiner was a disciple of theosophy, that branch of philosophy professing 'to attain to a knowledge of God by spiritual ecstacy, direct intuition or special individual relations.' He preached a cosmic creed and established a system of movement concerned with astral and occult ideas. He can be linked with Laban in that 'he stands squarely in the stream of cosmic beliefs that flow directly from ancient doctrines of harmony and flux' (Curl, 1967b). Most of Laban's early works have allusions to, and use of, ancient doctrines of harmony, the cosmos, crystals and circles. There is enough overlap in the thoughts of the two men to see that they are in the same school of thought and indicative of their times, class and culture.

Bienz has shown the involvement of Laban with Reuss, a close friend of Steiner, in a masonic connection. He also indicates Laban's interest, at that time, in theosophy and the work of Annie Besant in England. In fact, Laban's masonic ties have more in common with Steiner's theosophy than orthodox masonic craft rituals.

Steiner was in education long before Laban and used the art of eurhythmy as a psychological adjustment vehicle and for therapeutic purposes. Both these ideas are promulgated by Laban in his basic tracts.

Dalcroze links with Laban in the same way as many of those already discussed. As the links between them have similar ideological bases, the relationship is examined more specifically in the next part of the study. Here, it is only necessary to note Laban's visit to Hellarau when Dalcroze was working there. As a centre of the arts in Germany after World War I, Hellarau drew artists from all disciplines and the work there inspired many of them. Laban was no exception.

In 1926 Laban visited America. He was unimpressed by American culture at large but fascinated by the ritualistic movement of the American Indians. Also, at this time, he claims to have visited the Near-East and had 'unforgettable movement impressions'. What these were is not detailed but one could expect a man with Laban's interests, travelling in the Near East, and in Africa and China earlier according to two sources (Laban & Lawrence, 1947; Bruce, 1965) to have studied traditional dances of the Arabic culture, oriental dance forms, and temple dancing. There is no documentation of his responses to these experiences, but he did not accept them uncritically as art-forms because there is no evidence in his later work that he stylized them into his own productions. His later activities show that he found them too rigid, too organized in closed-systems with set end-products, for his own ideas. These observations provided him with the perfect vehicle against which to weigh his formulating ideas of basic movement principles.

Laban's interest in the work of Gurdjieff, verified by Bienz, also implies an interest in the activities outlined above.

It is worth developing this interest in Gurdjieff as it does shed some light on Laban the man and the influences on his thinking.

George Ivanovitch Gurdjieff was born in 1877 in Alexandropul, near the Persian Frontier of Russia. He is regarded as a Mystic and is the originator of a 'system' which bears his name. His followers are now formed into a cult, the tenets of which are derived from a study of Gurdjieff's writings, now available in two major books – *All and Everything: an objectively impartial criticism of the life of man, or Beelzebub's tales to his grandson,* and *Meetings with Remarkable Men,* both published by Routledge and Kegan Paul.

Gurdjieff is regarded as a philosopher by some but is probably better described as 'A Master', using the term as it is used in many Eastern cultures. This concept is indefinite and vague but it implies a teaching role and the possession of certain mystic knowledge which can be used to awaken other men and help them in their search for meaning in life simply by the master's presence.

His sytem is concerned with the fullest development of consciousness, and is based on the 'harmonious development of man'. Gurdjieff opened an Institute in Paris in 1922 to help further his studies and to provide a home for the movement which developed world-wide connections.

Gurdjieff can be compared to Laban in many ways. They were contemporaries, both were mystics and interested in eastern cultures and the teachings of eastern philosophers. They both used Movement as a means to spiritual understanding and were both concerned with cosmic structures and knowledge. Both attracted rich patrons who supported their endeavours and both achieved great prominence as exiles. Laban is often referred to as 'the master' and his work, like Gurdjieff's has spread throughout the world through the efforts of pupils and followers.

Gurdjieff is referred to in the text several times principally to show that Laban was drawn to his work and ideas and may have drawn on them in the development of his own ideas.

Laban's work in Germany between the wars set the scene for many ideas which have become associated with his English period. It was during this time that contact was first established between Laban and those English educationists who were instrumental in projecting his ideas on to the English educational scene. This development is taken up in detail in part three. Here it is appropriate to show that certain seeds germinated in Laban's early English students which bore fruit when he came to this country.

Sylvia Bodmer, a leading figure in Laban's Manchester days, and now President of the Laban Art of Movement Guild joined him in 1920 from Zurich, where she lived, when he was working in Stuttgart. She was later responsible for the movement-choir at the Frankfurt Opera House.

Lesley Burrowes had worked with Mary Wigman in Dresden. The latter declared her indebtedness to Laban in the testimony, 'seven long and hard years of study and work with Laban laid the foundation for my career as a dancer and dance educator'. Burrowes returned to form her own studio in London where one of her early pupils was Joan Goodrich of Bedford College of Physical Education. The latter recommended Diana Jordan to attend the Lesley Burrowes Studio. The first published work, concerned with movement education to appear in England was written by Diana Jordan and published by Oxford University Press in 1938. It was titled, *The Dance as Education,* and although not immediately influential, it was still pertinent to the problems educators faced after the war when its impact began to be felt. Diana Jordan, as Dance Organizer in the West Riding of Yorkshire, played an important role in implementing Laban's ideas in the education system (see part three).

Like many liberal progressives and free-thinkers in Germany in the 1930s, Laban found himself opposed to Nazi doctrines and tried to combat them. He represented the individual and the development of creative personal potential in a Germany where these things were anathema. When he came to England via Paris in 1938 he found people receptive to his ideas. His methods, principles, ideals and emphasis on free development were sucked into the mainstream of democratic fervour building up in England at that time. Gurdjieff's view that appropriate ideas are in the air for a particular climate of opinion, applies here. There were people in England who were receptive to Laban's ideas and reflective about them. His total philosophy did not preclude the latter. The system, if such it was, could be classified as 'open-ended'.

England 1938 - 1958

Laban arrived in England on 8 January 1938 and went to Dartington Hall where Kurt Jooss and Sigurd Leeder had established a dance school. Both these men, and Lisa Ullmann, who was also there, had worked with him in Germany. Laban was accepted into this rather intimate symposium as a 'Guru' figure. Leeder, at interview, referred to him as 'omniscient - the source of our inspiration - a movement genius.' The others shared this admiration. Lisa Ullmann in a similar interview reported:

> He found original thought in everything. He was an altruistic discoverer who produced ideas and let us develop them. He lifted us all out of our nineteenth-century dominated thinking.

There is great significance in the time which Laban spent at Dartington. In 1931, Leonard and Dorothy Elmhirst had founded Dartington as a trust which had both commercial and non-commercial activities concerned with the arts. The enterprise flourished and drew artists from several disciplines, many of whom were exiles from totalitarian oppression. As early as 1933, Jooss had to move from Germany. He desperately needed a refuge for himself and his group. The Elmhirsts, on the other hand were looking for an artist of international standard and experience, with a coherent philosophy of the dance (Bonham-Carter, 1958). It was, therefore, of mutual benefit that in 1934, Jooss came to Dartington.

Between 1934 and 1939, Dartington saw dancers with international reputations come and go. The Ballet Jooss was acquired by the Dartington Trustees. Michael Chekhov, nephew of Anton, directed the theatre studio, and such men as the painters Mark Tobey, Cecil Collins and Hein Heckroth; the sculptor Willi Soukop and the potter Bernard Leach were based there.

Into this circle came Laban as 'the master'. He experimented
with movement as a unifying element in the arts disciplines,
gave advice on the training schemes for reducing the physical
strain on estate workers, and generally imbibed the atmosphere
of living with this exceptional group of artists.

Laban had little knowledge of English Education in 1938.
The fact that his first home was at Dartington may be
important. Dartington had strong links with the main English
educational innovations of the time, and housed one of the
most famous English progressive schools. Its first headmaster,
William Burnlee Curry has been linked with Badley (Bedales)
and Neill (Summerhill) as the most prominent figures in
progressive education this century (Stewart, 1968). Dartington
was in the mainstream of progressive educational thought
characterized by the members of the New Education
Fellowship whose influences on imaginative approaches to
education have been marked.

The New Education Fellowship grew out of the meetings,
in 1914, of an informal group which took the title 'New Ideals
in Education'. Many of the educational innovators referred to
by Stewart (1968) belonged to this group. In 1920, the
Theosophical Fraternity arranged the first organized beginnings of the New Education Fellowship and used Beatrice
Ensor's journal, *The New Era in Home and School* to promote
the fellowship. It became an international institution and its
conferences generally explored concepts on the frontiers of
educational theory and practice. The fellowship has survived
internal rifts and has continued to provide a platform for
progressive innovation in Education. It was always sympathetic
to Laban's approaches to Movement Education and its
members supported the development of Laban's ideas in
English schools. Dalcroze, Jung, Sadler and Buber who are in
the Laban tradition were supporters of the fellowship, W. B.
Curry headmaster at Dartington was an active worker. It is not
an unreasonable hypothesis that Laban's ideas on the nature of
English education were influenced, during the early part of his
stay here, by sympathizers of the New Education Fellowship.
The regard of the fellowship for Laban's work was shown in
their tribute to him in *The New Era* (the foundation's
magazine) in 1959 after his death. Raymond O'Malley, who
was acting headmaster of Dartington Hall for a time,

differentiates between the Arts Centre and the School at Dartington. The progressive educational ideas were centred in the latter. O'Malley doubts whether much real influence from the New Education Fellowship tenets can be attributed to Laban's thinking on this account. At Dartington, Laban was quickly concerned with English educationists who learned from him and developed his work in the educational sphere. Leslie Burrowes, Diana Jordan, Ruth Foster and Lisa Ullmann were all immediately available to take advantage of Laban's presence. An expressionist ethos had been established at Dartington before Laban's arrival by Margaret Barr and, therefore, there was an 'accepting' climate for Laban's ideas. A favourable view of Laban's art was assured through the involvement in it by Beatrice Straight, the daughter of Dorothy Elmhirst by her first marriage. Besides Margaret Barr, Louise Soelberg also had enjoyed some success with a group of dancers working on experimental lines before Laban's arrival. Kurt Jooss came to Dartington indirectly through the good offices of Beryl de Zoete who had connections with the arts at Dartington. So Laban came into a vibrant movement community when he arrived at Dartington. He was not an initiator here but one of many artists helping to make Dartington a great cultural centre. It is doubtful whether Laban would have had such a direct and immediate educational impact if the Dartington ethos had not existed, and if he had not become a part of it for a time on his arrival in England. Many other refugees from Nazi persecution came to England but did not receive early recognition and subsequently continued their journeys and eventually settled in America. Most had moved so often that in 1938 they felt just as insecure in England as they had done previously on the continent. America, to them, was a haven out of the reach of tyranny. Laban, however, stayed and his first early students were able to offer such expansion of his ideas through Education that Laban himself became very much in demand, even during the war years when he was officially registered as an alien. In many ways Dartington set the ethos for his later work.

When Laban arrived in England to be greeted as 'the master' by his former dance fraternity, the education world was ignorant of his work in the main. It is significant that in the only published work in England linking Dance and Education (Jordan, 1938) there is no mention of Laban by name. Although Jordan had been indirectly influenced previously by Laban, she does not acknowledge this influence in 1938. In a later publication (Jordan 1966), however, she pays a specific, glowing tribute to the influence of Laban on the creative development of physical education in England in the early 1940s. We must accept from what she says:

> Rudolph Laban's work had already preceded him in this country, and there were one or two teachers who had discovered something about it through artists and teachers who had trained in Europe.

> Throughout the war, an increasing number of women teachers were able to develop this understanding of Laban's deep and wide life-time study of movement.

that Laban was having an immediate, if small impact on English Education shortly after his arrival in this country.

When Laban came to England he was very ill, thin and undernourished. He had no money and indeed, his friends already here were comparatively poor. This situation meant that the initial courses undertaken by Laban and Ullman in England provided a significant source of income and were an economic necessity. No doubt, the educational interest was sincere but the financial aspect was also a motivation at this time. What the attitude to the courses would have been if offers of opportunity to work more with Dance as an art form had been forthcoming is pure speculation. Would Laban have entered the educational field by choice? A look at his career to date suggests that he would not. Thus do these unplanned influences affect future action.

Laban's first studio was acquired in Manchester. It was dingy and in many ways unsuitable, but it was a base from which his work could develop. Educationists went there and left to encourage his ideas in their work in schools. Another feature of the time in Manchester, was that Laban was able to work again as a Movement Consultant. In this work, he followed the advice of Noverre and studied the work habits of people. He developed his early ideas on the analysis and use of movement in work in Switzerland before 1920, and advised on industrial problems concerned with workers' movements in

Germany in the 1930s. In England he was introduced by Sir William Slater, then the Secretary of the Agricultural Research Council, to Mr F. C. Lawrence, an industrial consultant in Manchester. With Lawrence, Laban undertook the detailed observation of the movement of women employed in a wartime factory moving large tyres. From this work they published the book *Effort* (Laban & Lawrence, 1947) which codified the bases of many of their experiments. Alongside his psychological observation of industrial movement, Laban was developing and refining his system of movement notation which was used extensively to record and define the movements of his subjects. Lawrence has paid many tributes to Laban's genius in the field of movement consultancy in industry and documented how present-day systems draw on Laban's early inquiries. The most direct link between Laban's early work and the sophisticated movement study techniques used in industry today is through Warren Lamb. In his book *Posture and Gesture,* Lamb acknowledges his indebtedness to Laban, and shows that he has drawn heavily on Laban's ideas. Since the publication of this book in 1965, Lamb has achieved international fame as a movement consultant and has attracted the attention of the mass media who have reported his work in detail on many occasions. The chief interest of the media has been in Lamb's action profiles of managers based on a type of non-verbal communication. This approach is still regarded as original by personnel selection experts. Lamb described it as 'like acupuncture in management'. It draws on Laban's basic principles and follows up Laban's early ideas on the relationship of posture and gesture to personality characteristics.

The Laban-Lawrence Test for 'Selection and Placing' is still in use in personnel selection but since Laban's death, the Studio has been more concerned with movement in Education than industry. Laban's industrial work has been developed more by former pupils working as free-lance agents.

The work of Laban developed and extended in the 1950s, especially when he achieved the stability of a home at the Studio in Addlestone in 1953. At this time, his main English writings were published and his ideas became more systematized and organized, in so far as this was possible in the light of his philosophy – 'it was characteristic of Laban's teaching, never to give concrete answers' (LAMG Magazine, December 1954). Much of the story of Laban's life at this time is inextricably bound up with how his ideas were translated into action in the schools. This is developed in part three.

No view of 'Laban – the man' can be complete without referring specifically to the personal recollection of those who knew him well.

In the research for this publication, many men and women who had worked with Laban, and whose subsequent careers had taken them to positions of responsibility in their particular disciplines, were interviewed. One of the features of the interview was to try to ascertain whether Laban exhibited the personality characteristics said by psychologists to be associated with high creatives. It turned out that Laban was regarded by his contemporaries and pupils as an archetypal creative personality. They thought he was intelligent, original, independent, receptive, intuitive, sensitive and resolute.

In general conversation, these same characteristics were often mentioned, but in rather more conversational phrases:

'His students were in awe of him' (Jordan)

'He was unpredictable' (Knust)

'He knew where he was going' (Leeder)

'He talked with immense authority' (Dunn)

'He had an air of inner calm and was very sensitive to the needs and problems of students when he acted as examiner' (Casson)

'A very original thinker' (Bodmer)

'He once said to me, "In 200 years time they will understand".' (Ullmann)

'He exuded power' (Preston-Dunlop)

'Intuitively, he knew what the educationists around him needed and he supplied it' (Preston-Dunlop)

One method of studying creative activities is to take acknowledged 'high-creatives' and make a detailed analysis of their individual cognitive styles, methods of working, essential cues to creative endeavour, and the environments which seemed to facilitate the production of creative ideas (Ghiselin, 1955). A similar technique was adopted in this inquiry with data built up from interviews. There is evidence to support the view of 'Laban – a creative personality'. Reference was made earlier to the contradictory nature of the man – but this complexity may have contributed to his production of creative ideas. From his archives, it appears that he was an avid writer – but many of these writings are jottings, notes, scribblings, half-formed ideas to be worked on later. In many cases, they never were developed or edited. Leeder described Laban as 'an ideas man', 'a beginner', 'an originator who handed on his ideas for other people to develop.' Valerie Preston-Dunlop contributes to this view. He often handed over to her complex problems concerned with his movement ideas which she was unable to handle. She calls his attitude 'irresponsible' at times, and thinks he had a disregard for the future of his work. He made no attempt to control his ideas. He was generous with them and made no effort to keep them for personal gain or glory.

Many colleagues told of his disorganized way of working, his reluctance to be definitive in his views, instructional techniques, and in the way his work should be interpreted. This is often the behaviour of a highly creative person. 'They can live easily with an unsolved problem.' 'They accept disorder and are stimulated by it.' 'They make mistakes, are independent, self-starters, willing to take risks . . .' (Torrance, 1962). The evidence gained from analysing the interview data was that all the Torrance statements quoted applied to Laban.

Laban emerges as a complex personality, often showing paradoxical qualities. His personality profile fits in with current views on the creative personality. In a recently published study by Storr (1972), the conclusion is that:

> Our picture of the creative individual is gradually taking shape as a person who possesses an unusual combination of qualities, rather than one particular attribute. It is the tension between these opposites and the need to resolve this tension which provide the motive force for creation.

The latter point is true of Laban. Much of his basic theory rests on a concept of polarity and the resolving of tensions to achieve new levels of creative satisfaction.

Laban had many of the attributes said to be associated with

the creative personality. This is important. What would have been his attitude towards Movement Education today? Would he have modified his theories in the light of changing life-styles? Would he have eschewed any rigidity of approach said to have his work as its basis? If we accept that his personality was as it has been detailed here, it is likely that 'change' would have characterized his approach. Flexibility and elaboration would have been his watchwords, and an on-going, intensive progression would have been his desire. These ideas, presented here initally, require examination in the context of the current education scene in England. This is done in part three.

Laban died on 1 July 1958. Tribute was paid to him in the Laban Art of Movement Guild Magazine in November 1958 and throughout the education press at that time. His position as one of the greatest theoreticians of dance and human movement was shown and critics from the world of the Dance were lavish in their appreciations of his contributions to the art.

Kirstein (1969), the Dance historian wrote:

> Laban was a powerful, infused individualistic dance-composer. He was a Nietzchean theorist, a Wagnerian innovator dedicated to quasi-mystical attempts to enforce the unique supremacy of movement as movement. His researches towards the direction of movement he called 'Eukinetek' indicating a preoccupation with motion as against Dalcroze's 'Eurhythmic'.

It is significant that practically all the comment after his death concerned Laban and the Dance. Indeed, a consistent view of some commentators on the physical education scene who were close to Laban is that he remained essentially 'a man of the theatre' (Munrow, 1972). He was a late entrant into the educational world. His entry would probably have surprised his colleagues in the Dance world. There is an element of chance in the way Laban had his interests directed towards Education.

PART TWO
IDEOLOGICAL DEBTS

A study of Laban's life and his ideas reveals a wealth of ideological debts. These are more easily analysed if they are grouped and considered under these generic headings:

1 Laban's principles
2 General foundations
3 Mysticism
4 Psychological bases
5 Artistic roots
6 Architecture and freemasonry
7 Scientific thought

Laban's principles
Laban regarded Movement as an art and a philosophy and indeed describes himself once as a dance-poet (Laban, 1935). He saw the Art of Movement as an end in itself, and an 'elixir of life'. All his writings stress these aspects. He was not intrinsically interested in Movement as an educational tool and vehicle.

His work rests on five fundamental ideas which cannot be said to be 'educational'. They are:

(i)   Dance as a divine power
(ii)   The Reigen or Circle - Dance
(iii)   Unity and Ecstasy
(iv)   The Crystal
(v)   Harmony (Curl, 1967a)

His thinking was predominantly dance-orientated and only part of his work has ideas with educational significance.

Before studying specifics, it is worth examining the concept of polarity which is seen as the essence of Laban's work (Bodmer, 1960). The following polar ideas are important and at the base of his thinking:

> stable and labile equilibrium
> counter movements of body parts
> symmetry and asymmetry
> central and peripheral orientation
> growing and shrinking
> recurrence and free rhythmicality
> relatedness and relationship corollaries
> inner and outer concepts
> that all movements have a complementary action

These ideas are by no means original. Huxley (1961) in a general philosophical discourse makes the same generalization when he asserts:

> On all levels of our being, from the muscular and sensational, to the moral and intellectual, every tendency generates its own opposite . . . We will a movement; one set of muscles is stimulated and, automatically, by spinal induction, the opposing muscles are inhibited. Every yes begets a corresponding no.

In Huxley's work, which presents a similar idea to that expressed by Laban, there is also something of the Freudian concept of reaction-formation.

Another way of studying Laban's ideas is to examine the impact which his ideas may make on people. This approach suggests that those trained through his principles:

1 Picture the structure of the human creature as related to movement in space.

2 Appreciate the harmonic relation of body weight to gravity, a relation that explains tension and relaxation.

3 Accept rhythm as a function of the human body.

4 Understand how the intellectual concepts of time, measure, phrase etc., emerge from rhythm (Kennedy, 1950).

The essential features of Laban's work are mirrored in the effect it is said they have on individuals. The inference that movement education is a basic training for all activities of life is a central theme of educationists who use Laban's work.

Comprehensive reviews of the nature of Laban's theories are numerous (Curl, 1967a; Redfern, 1973; Thornton, 1971) and it is not the intention to repeat these descriptive tracts. Those with particular significance for this study are discussed in appendix two. To see how others influenced Laban and to judge the educational impact of his work, however, it is necessary to detail some main facets of his work.

Fundamentally, Laban made an analysis of human movement and its meaning and application to art, education, therapy, recreation, and industry. The aim of his work was to assist the harmonization of the individual through the Art of Movement by giving him insights and a heightened perception of consciousness into his physical, intellectual, emotional and spiritual relationship and inter-dependencies. His discoveries have been summarized in five statements:

(i) That all human movement has two purposes, functional and expressive.

(ii) That dancing is symbolic action.

(iii) That all movement of a part or parts of the body is composed of discernable factors that are common to men everywhere. These factors are contained in two overall terms: effort and shape.

(iv) That there are inherent movement patterns of effort and shape which are indicative of harmonious movement.

(v) A system of notation that makes it possible to record accurately all movement of the human body (Gaumer, 1960).

'Laban did not have an analysis of movement' (Preston-Dunlop, 1967b). This radical opinion from one of his most distinguished students shows that in her view, he provided new lines of thought and produced more of a classification than an analysis. 'He was a synthesist in that he constantly searched for and found relationships.' Her use of synthesis re-affirms views expressed about Laban's creative personality attributes. The need to synthesize and to seek symbolic solutions is believed to be a basic human motivation especially associated with high creatives (Storr, 1972). This is an important statement, because the nexus of the role which others played in influencing Laban was to provide the material for his syntheses. It is a mark of his creative thinking that he saw unusual relationships, and brought together diverse frames of reference using the technique described by Arthur Koestler as 'bisociation'. Similarly, Preston-Dunlop draws attention to Laban's role as a catalyst. It is unwise to dwell on the actual content of his work because 'he himself was an initiator, not a completer'. He certainly innovated from the ideas of others as has been shown, but innovation cannot occur in a vacuum. The source of innovation is in experience and indeed, much of Laban's work arises from his 'inspired observation' of the work of others.

However we define Laban's principles; whether it is in terms of a classification, model, system, theory, synthesis, or code, it was firmly dance and art-form orientated in the first instance. One of the fascinations of the Laban story is the transition of a set of ideas, founded in one discipline, and receiving perhaps a greater approbation ultimately in another.

In summary, one of the major features of Laban's principles was an attempt to define logically, in finite terms, a set of bases for concepts whose nature is and whose boundaries are infinite.

General foundations

The thinking of Laban is in a great German tradition. While it breaks new ground in its delineation of movement principles, it can be shown to be very much influenced by the great German poets, thinkers and scientists who form part of what Runes (1959) calls 'the literary tradition'. In this phase he summed up movements covering a wide range of disciplines where ideas concerned with aesthetics were paramount.

Polarity and dualism are at the heart of most of the great German philosophies and were at the centre of Laban's thinking. Hegel, who also influenced Dewey, developed a philosophical system which tried to synthesize antagonistic tendencies. His ideas concerned with the conflict of thesis and antithesis which he called dialectics are ones which Laban uses to try to explain both human and cosmic reason.

Romantics such as Fichte express ideas very similar to Laban's. Fichte, whose work anticipated that of Kierkegaard, Heidegger and Nietzsche, was interested in the development of personality and showed the role of movement in realizing self-expression. On questions of self-expression Laban is probably closer to Fichte than Hegel; the latter supported the view that self-expression is only a partial reflection of the true self, while Fichte thought that in self-expression the true-self was revealed in full.

Laban's concern in many of his writings with unity and ecstasy is also understandable and predictable. Ecstasy was the essence of expressionism with which Laban was associated through his involvement in Dadaism which grew out of the expressionist movement (Willett, 1970). Also, Laban's interest in China and Chinese culture is in the expressionist tradition. The whole Expressionist generation in Germany had this love of China and was influenced by the writings of Laotse and K'ung Futse.

Laban (1935; 1960) was often preoccupied in his writings with the concepts of light and darkness and the relationship between these two states. The genealogy of this idea is not a unitary strand. The concept is also seen in Nietzsche's writings and is linked with the Apollonian view concerned with the God of Wisdom (light) on the one hand, and the Dionysian view concerned with the God of orgiastic mysticism (darkness) on the other. In this analogy, reason is linked with light, and orgy and ritual is coupled with darkness. Dalcroze, whose work is linked with Laban in detail later, was also concerned with the Apollonian/Dionysian idea. He says (Sadler, 1912):

> The dance could also be made to serve to express the Dionysian side of artistic expression, while Music conveys the Apollonian side or conversely, sounds could reproduce the frenzy of elemental passions in sensorial language while the dance embodied their decorative forms in space. In the one, as in the other case, we should achieve a spiritualisation of matter, a pure expression of soul, an idealization of form, and an emotionisation of sensation.

The Dalcroze idea serves to emphasize the use of this myth by several thinkers in the artistic field. Laban was not alone in his use of this form of explanation.

The Apollonian/Dionysian concept can be applied to Laban's whole philosophy in dance and education. His was an Apollonian view which admired and advocated purity, beauty and positive acceptance of the offerings of others. It can be contrasted with the Dionysian view of actively questioning any emergent ideas, opposing them initially on principle or assuming that new ideas must have complete validation before acceptance. The latter have something in common with 'the black paper' philosophy; the former are more akin to the ideas of the New Education Fellowship, and the educational progressives.

It is possible to show a sympathy between Laban and Rousseau. The latter thought that it was through movement that the child learned 'the difference between the self and the not self', and that through movement he discovered the concept of space. This idea is very much akin to Laban's thinking. They are in a lineage but whether Rousseau directly influenced Laban is speculative. Similarly Guts Muths, 'the grandfather of German gymnastics', stressed the importance of linking physical activity with 'the education of the head and the heart'; an idea found throughout Laban's thinking, i.e. that movement stimulates intellectual activity and problem-solving. The relationship here is just as speculative as that suggested for Rousseau. In the same way, Pestalozzi's 'natural' as distinct from his 'art' gymnastics, (where the emphasis was on the development of the innate capacities of the child), can be linked with Laban's ideas.

More direct ties can be established with Froebel. The basic tenets of Laban's philosophy can be linked to Froebel's concept of Darstellung – 'creative self-expression' (the satisfaction of an innate urge to push out to a greater life and to adjust to a greater unity). Basically, the idea is that:

> It is from the natural out-going of the child that we develop the art of movement, an art within the capacity of every individual, and an art which is capable of fulfilling Froebel's principles (Russell, 1958).

This view of Russell's makes fundamental assumptions concerned with the nature of basic human motivation which would be unacceptable to some. It is, however, a view widely accepted by progressive educators.

Froebel's concept that there is an inner connection between the mind and things perceived, and between feeling, thought and soul (making the inner outer) is very similar to Laban's view of the inherent harmony which man searches for. Laban believed that this harmony once achieved manifested itself openly in natural integration of effort and shape in human movement. Even stronger links are suggested between Laban and Froebel by both Curl (1969) and Russell (1958) who say that they both had vague idealistic philosophies; were dreamy, contemplative, followed pantheistic doctrines, were influenced by German idealists, and were strongly drawn to the teaching of Plato. The inference is that these attributes were in some way less than desirable but is this necessarily so? In his evaluation of Laban's work Curl adopts a devastating analytical technique which may be rather harsh when applied to the somewhat mystic and romantic ideas of Laban. In a letter, Laban's daughter, Juana asks:

> Is this piecemeal breakdown of everything Laban wrote the most suitable way to study the essence of his work? It is not the best idea to take all my father's thinking apart and dissect it.

She thinks a reflective approach is to be preferred. A case can be made to show relationships between the thinking of Froebel and Laban. Whether this implies a deliberate attempt on Laban's part to use Froebel's ideas is very doubtful. The position is probably that Laban was aware of Froebelianism and found himself sympathetic to the basic ideals.

KINETOGRAPHY is a system of notation that makes it possible to record accurately all movements of the human body (Laban, 1966). Discussing his work on this subject, Laban acknowledges his use of the work of others. He says:

> . . . the system itself was inspired by that of Beauchamp and Feuillet (around 1700) and was mainly evolved alongside my investigations of the various branches of choreosophia (an ancient Greek word from choros meaning circle and sophia meaning knowledge or wisdom).

He incorporated some of the ballet principles from Feuillet's *Art d'Ecrire la Dance,* in his first attempt to produce a system of notation (Brown & Sommer, 1969).

Although Laban does not give particular names, he does acknowledge his debt to osteology which he claims to have studied:

> This art has taught me to see the causes which oppose themselves in the execution of this or that movement, and knowing the bony structure of man and the levers and hinges which govern its play. (Laban 1954a).

The study of the mechanisms of movement is clearly linked with his ideas outlined earlier when the work of Bodmer, Huxley and Gaumer was quoted.

Comparisons can be drawn between Ling and Laban. Both pioneers were influenced by the natural philosophy of ancient Greeks and were concerned for the harmonization of the individual and the recognition of body and mind as a unity. Ling provided a base from which Laban could develop. The development which has stemmed from Laban could not have taken place without the liberalization which occurred through the influence of Ling.

Laban was a man of his time and a creative artist in the widest sense. He was a central European, born into an upper-class family whose travels took him to the centres of artistic thought during times of great debate concerning the nature of aesthetic experience. He was connected with liberal thinking communities and progressive ideas throughout the early years of this century and was in essence a true 'Bohemian'. He mixed with artists from many disciplines and his ideas can be seen in the work of his contemporaries in other arts. This pattern, where the creator in any discipline draws on the ideas of others working in different disciplines and with other media is common in the arts. A well-known magazine of the arts, *Leonardo* gives examples of this phenomenon in every issue. Laban often worked with those who drew their inspiration in some measure from their peers. In a similar manner, the work of Cizek, Reinhardt, Stanislavsky, Orff, Steiner and Hahn has been brought together in a mainstream of enlightened thinking by Richardson (1967). Because of the links made with Education, it seems desirable to quote this work fully:

> When teachers stop looking only for the routine responses, what they liberate themselves and their pupils from is the set of academic disciplines that have emerged over the centuries as a result of work done by artists and scientists on the frontiers of knowledge and creative experience. This is what Cizek was doing in Vienna when he freed his pupils from rules and

regulations and set them to paint out of their own imagination. This is what Stanislavsky did with his drama students in Moscow when he made them use their own feelings in a situation rather than obey rules of stage procedure and follow theatrical convention. This is what Rudolph Laban was doing when he based his work with dancers on fundamental experiences of movement rather than on techniques learned second-hand from other dancers. This is what Carl Orff was doing with children at the Guentherschule in Munich when he helped them to discover from the examination of their own speech tunes and rhythms, that melody and metrical patterns were part of their own natural equipment and not mere inventions of the musicologists.

All these revolutions - in the teaching of art, drama, dance and music - were beginning in the twenties. What use have our schools been able to make of these innovations?

The final question is examined subsequently. Here, the aim is to show that Laban was part of a questioning, liberalizing movement, common to the work of some central Europeans in the early years of this century. He belonged to this genre and took up much of its ethos. Besides 'taking up' the ethos, however, he did innovate from it. Dancers previously had not been known for their thinking powers but Laban was a thinker who formulated serious theories at this time about movement, rhythm and the body. In spite of his inflated style and 'mixed-metaphysics', he has to be taken seriously as a thinker. His ideas concerned with the theatre, however, were often received with caution at first. Germany was not a ballet nation in the Russian tradition and so German commentators viewed all dance, whether classical or modern with some reserve. Salient features of German dance at this time included a concentration on the solo dance, dancing in the near-nude (pseudo-Greek style), and the development of the chorus. They were all influenced by the thinking and teaching of Laban. They, in their turn, influenced him.

Mysticism
Curl (1968, 1969) argues that Plato and Pythagoras had a significant influence on Laban's theories. In fact, he concludes:

Without philosophical training, the confusion of mystical metaphysics of Laban's works must to the student seem insuperable; but one major clue has enabled us to give the whole of Laban's writings an orientation. This is their affinity with Pythagorean doctrine and thought. Here, as nowhere else, lies the explanation for otherwise incomprehensible theory.

His main support for this view comes from the use of 'pseudo-mathematical symbolism based on archetypal crystals and cosmic circularity'. Curl builds up strong links between Pythagorean theory and Laban's work. It is conjectural whether the emphasis which Curl places on this is justifiable. Laban uses Pythagorean ideas but these are not the sole basis for his thinking. Curl shows similarities between their thinking and compares their ideas. This is good academic study but only that and nothing more. He offers hypotheses rather than conclusions and his ideas must remain as interesting opinion rather than proven fact.

One can draw comparisons between Laban's use of ideal forms and the Platonic theory of forms. However, this concept is a persistent notion which runs through the work of many men who were associated with high idealism and philosophies of nature. Both Goethe and Schiller used the Platonic view of ideal forms in their work.

Curl attributes Laban's ideas almost totally to Platonic and Pythagorean bases but this is surely a narrow view. Laban is more 'a man of his time' whose ideas represent a whole spectrum of current thought and who developed his ideas from this as well as drawing on earlier ideas. Contemporary thought at large may have been influenced by Plato. Laban must be seen as part of a movement owing something to Plato but he was not a narrow Platonic disciple.

Laban's views on cosmic power have been attributed to Plato (Curl, 1967a; Lange, 1969) but Hegel also formulated principles concerning cosmic reason which he believed:

> . . . operates within the soul of man whose consciousness is the area of the subjective spirt, while the objective spirit becomes manifest in cultural and social institutions like law and morality, and the absolute spirit can be grasped in the arts, religion and philosophy.

Laban's view of dance as a divine power is usually linked with his search for what Hegel would have called the absolute spirit. The concept of 'search' is important. Hegel put becoming above being but Laban saw dance as the process (becoming) which initiated the evolution which led to being. In this way, Laban was using current ideas and innovating from them.

Laban also studied the work of Gurdjieff and Ouspensky (see Part One). There is much in common between Laban and Gurdjieff. They were contemporary, and were both mystics. Gurdjieff was concerned with self-knowledge and the search for ultimate understanding. He believed that people had the ability to release very high level energy which enabled them to make revelations about themselves. In order to achieve a state where this could be done, Gurdjieff required his followers to undertake movement which was based on temple-dancing. Gurdjieff, like Laban was influenced by Sufi, the Dervish culture, and the mystics of the east. This link is another indication of Laban seeking out mystical knowledge. There is little in common between the stereotyped temple-dancing used in the Gurdjieff system to attain a high-level of attention, and the movement associated with Laban. The connection is a common interest in mysticism.

Mr J. G. Bennett, a world authority on Gurdjieff and Ouspensky and now Principal of the Institute for the Comparative Study of History, Philosophy and the Sciences at Sherborne elaborated on the links between Laban and these two men. Both Bennett and Mrs Nott, an early associate of Gurdjieff thought that there were links between them. Bennett believed that the links were through Dalcroze. There were no works of either Gurdjieff or Ouspensky available in Switzerland during the time Laban was there. If Bienz is right about Laban's study of Gurdjieff's work, it would have been through contact with a pupil or someone having knowledge of his ideas. Many emigrées came from Russia to Switzerland at that time. This is the mostly likely source of Laban's knowledge of Gurdjieff in 1916–20. The links through Dalcroze would be later than these dates when Gurdjieff's work was published in Western Europe. There are ideological links between the work of Laban and Gurdjieff. Both men searched for mystic knowledge and had common philosophical interests. They saw movement as an essential feature in the attainment of a high level of functioning and creative self-expression.

Laban's movement principles have been compared with a pack of Tarot playing cards and their mystical symbolism by North (1964a). Tarot means a royal path and the Tarot cards chart the direction of one's life, materially and spiritually. Its disciples accord them the highest occult powers and maintain that they suggest accurate prediction of mental therapy and spiritual development. The cards are 'as old as Babylon'. They cross-reference with astrology and zodiac signs, with numerology and the world's greatest religions and myths (Cilento, 1972). The suggested connection with the Tarot cards is summed up in the passage:

> I shall not be so bold as to try to relate Laban's analysis of movement content, his effort elements, drives and attitudes, directly to the (Tarot) interpretations, or to the colours and directional signs incorporated in the symbols, though there are some analogies which are difficult to avoid.

The view of this connection is very much akin to many of Curl's arguments. They are suppositions based on the study of two artefacts which have an overt connection. A dependence is then suggested which may be tenable but there is no real evidence that once influenced the other at its inception. However, drawing together the mystical elements of Tarot and Laban's own mysticism is of some academic interest. Similarly, elements of Laban's principles can be seen in the art of movement as it existed in ancient China. Perhaps this is a more legitimate connection as Laban does acknowledge his interest in movement in ancient China in several of his guild magazine articles.

Psychological bases
Many of Laban's pronouncements have a Freudian ring. In his light/darkness article already referred to, he says:

> Seen from the reality of wake-state, the dream is full of symbols. In a symbol, the inner essence of things and happenings is captured. This means that dreams and their symbols have a certain proximity to the space (of the body) world.

This passage, containing as it does, the basic idea of Freudian dream-interpretation indicates an awareness in Laban's writings of Freud's work and its implications for movement study. He continues . . . 'so do devotion, surrender, abandon, in which the "I" is dying.' The Freudian view of the nature of the ego is implicit here in the same way as the other concept. However, one could suggest that 'surrender in which the "I" is dying' owes more to Dervish dance and other Eastern methods of achieving total surrender of the self than to Freudian ideas of the Ego. Since Laban (1947) acknowledges both influences, their joint effect can be assumed. Similarly, Laban's use of dream symbols may be nearer to Tarot than Freud; more akin to astrology than psychology! There are other Freudian links but these are dealt with in the context of justifying Movement Education later.

At interview, Diana Jordan, talked about a correspondence which Laban had conducted with Jung. Apparently, he was intensely interested in Jung's work, and appeared to think that there were common elements in their thinking. This is another case where at this time, 'ideas were in the air'. A range of thinkers in different disciplines were studying the nature of human behaviour and presenting similar views.

Jung was concerned with the way humans express innate potential through their encounters with their environment. He called this process 'individuation' (becoming an individual) and described it as 'a vast spectrum in life's meaning which cannot be articulated in rational terms but which de-mands expression.' This is exactly what Laban believes happens through a study of movement, and subsequent expression which emanates from that study. It is a common idea in the movement field – expressed by Martha Graham as that which 'comes from inner nature and goes into experience'.

The work of Jung greatly influenced thinkers in the arts who were looking for a theory of aesthetics and a rationale for their creative endeavours. He was probably more important than Freud:

> . . . in the interpretation of those super-individual or collective phenomenon which take the form of myth or symbol and are so much involved in expression (Read, 1943).

His concern was to explain the role of symbolism in behaviour and to make links between this concept, and myth and expression. The affinity of this concern to Laban's basic ideals can be deduced.

Jung searched for wholeness and represented the wholeness of meaningful spiritual experiences in symbolic forms. Many of the drawings which he made to help express his thinking were similar to those made by Laban and now in the archives. They are characteristic of ideas concerned with the gestalt which were common in a variety of disciplines during the early years of this century.

Jung refers a great deal to the shadow in an individual's subconscious and uses this shadow symbolically in the same way that Laban uses the concept of darkness in his light/darkness article. Another idea common to the two men was in the realm of the metaphysical. They both expressed the view that the psyche in part was not confined to space and time. Both were mystics who approached their search for the soul from their own interests, Jung using depth analysis and Laban using kineasthetic experience. Laban's correspondence with Jung shows his interest in the latter's activities. The similarity of many of their ideas puts them in the same philosophical 'cell'. Attempts to link Laban and Jung through meetings held at the Casa Ehrenos have proved unfruitful. At Casa Ehrenos, meetings were held where acknowledged experts concerned with current problems conducted seminars for their contemporaries. Laban was resident near Ascona at this time and one can assume he would have been interested in these meetings. Attempts to verify this have been unsuccessful.

In a later section, the psychological justification for the role of the art of movement in Education is examined. Now, the influence of the gestalt psychologists on Laban during his early life is analysed. Laban (1961) acknowledges his awareness of their work. He shows a particular interest in the work of Köhler and refers extensively to it in relation to the dancing of apes. This was material he originally used in 1939. There are earlier indications of psychological work which was very much in line with his thinking. As early as 1912, Lipps was developing a theory of Empathy which introduced a concept of direct association between expressive movements and a state of mind – a theory very much in the Froebel tradition referred to earlier. Many of the gestalt psychologists were concerned with the relationship of movement to behaviour. Wertheimer, in his book *Productive Thinking* connects kinaesthetics and thinking. Wolff (1945) relates gesture, morphology of the hand and constitutional tendencies, temperament and mentality. She regards gestures as indicative of social attitudes and states of mind, and suggests positive correlations between specific gestures and certain types of personality. These are regular ideas encountered in all Laban's books, and the basis of the ideas which were taken up by Warren Lamb (1964) working in industry.

The basic gestalt concepts of unity and form and the search for these in human behaviour are part of a way of thinking which characterized intellectuals in the early years of this century although, of course, the same concepts had concerned Plato in *The Republic*. Laban was part of the movement which explored these ideas; a movement which contained a wide spectrum of intellectuals across Western Europe during the first quarter of this century.

Read (1943) shows that the Gestalt school influenced the arts over a wide field:

> The application of Gestalt psychology to aesthetics has proceeded slowly but no firmer ground has ever been won . . .

The importance of kinaesthetic activity in the development of sensory experience is implicit in this statement which was written about 1940. Laban had been aware of this and used it in the 1920s.

Artistic roots

At interview, one name repeatedly cropped up in answer to the question, 'Who do you think may have influenced Laban in his own thinking?' This was Jean George Noverre (1727-1809), the ballet-master who had immense influence on art and music in his time. One of his descendants documents the field of the man's activities – 'Noverre was notable not only on account of his productions, and of the improvements which he introduced into his art, but for his connection with celebrated personages . . . Among crowned heads, Frederick the Great, Marie-Thérèse and Marie-Antoinette; among musicians, Gluck, Puccini, Mozart, Mazzinghi, Haydn and Cherubini; among actors David Garrick; and among men of literature Diderot and Voltaire' (Noverre, 1882). He was thought of as a dangerous innovator and scorner of orthodox custom; a man who wished to rid the dance world of its rigid formality and narrow inflexibility. Many of Noverre's ideas are echoed by Laban including his concern with 'beautiful nature', his common rule that imitation should lead to creative synthesis rather than stop at servile copy, his rejection of ballet forms ('the five positions are good to know but better to forget') (Lyncham, 1950) and his concern with philosophising about the dance.

Laban acknowledges his debt to Noverre in the first edition of the Guild Magazine and develops the theme that movement study has concerned man throughout the ages and continues:

> I will mention in this connection Jean George Noverre, who, as early as the eighteenth century, had visions of dispensing with the artificialities and cramping formality of the movement of his time as he saw it in the dances of the court circles. He told his pupils to go out into the streets and market squares to watch the people in their everyday actions.

It is this latter point which Laban borrowed from Noverre; the observation of natural movement to elucidate further knowledge. However, several other links can be made. Noverre's use of the word 'art', when he is referring to the need for a full understanding of movement is in the tradition of Laban's work (Stephenson, 1960). Laban's interest in Noverre as a teacher is not new. John Morey, a dancing master in Doncaster went to London to study Noverre's teaching techniques. He became a Noverre pupil and influenced many other teachers of the time in the Yorkshire area particularly (Harrison, 1957).

Laban's focus on unity, already linked with Froebel, also was a constant theme of Noverre. The Aristotelian view that events are not subject to a unity of time, place and action but are more bound by a unity of design was propounded by Noverre and is always in the forefront of Laban's thinking. Similarly, Noverre's concern with gesture and its influence on personality and character ('This stance, this deportment, this way of moving, always common to his trade and always pleasing . . .') was taken up by Laban and written up in detail by one of his pupils, Warren Lamb, in his book *Posture and Gesture*, where he shows his great indebtedness to Laban.

The activities of Loie Fuller merit mention. She danced in Paris at the time Laban lived there. She was a precursor of Isadora Duncan (of whom, more later) and revived interest in Greek and Roman drama and movement. Her work is detailed in a contemporary journal, *Strand Magazine Vol. 7 1894* where it was pointed out that she was concerned with natural movements and had considerable influence on the emergence of new art forms at the time. (See also Hall 1953). It is inconceivable that Laban would have been unacquainted with her work and its implications for his own inquiries. Loie Fuller was interested in the control of light and the use of light in architecture. These facets featured strongly in her stage design and sets. Also, she put movement before music in her choreography and stressed that movement was the expression of a sensation, an idea she develops in her own autobiography (Fuller 1913). Her links between movement sensation and expression put her in the Laban syndrome. Also, she had close contacts with other great names in related disciplines. Rodin was her associate. Anatole France wrote the introduction to her book, *Fifteen years of a dancer's life*. She was in the mainstream of new thinking in the arts, in Paris, when Laban was there.

Most commentators on Laban to date have suggested that Laban's work owes something to Delsarte. There are similarities particularly in a relationship between Delsarte's logical system of expressive movement and Laban's analysis (Craus, 1969). Laban used some of Delsarte's terminology and developed his ideas on 'oppositions', 'parallelisms', and 'successions'. Delsarte's teaching was the first to reveal what modern dancers call 'tension and relaxation', or 'contraction and release': thus it was he who laid the foundation for the German modern dance which in turn strongly influenced American modern dance (Shawn, 1963). Claims have been made that Laban studied with a pupil of Delsarte but the pupil is not named (Kraus, 1946).

The colleagues of Laban who were interviewed nearly all specifically mentioned Delsarte when discussing those who may have influenced Laban. The only exception was Lisa Ullmann who categorically stated that Laban owed nothing to Delsarte. She was unable to say clearly why she believed this. She seemed to feel that Laban regarded Delsarte's work as having been systematized too soon. However, there is a case for accepting that Laban was influenced by Delsarte, the most pressing part of which seems to be use of similar terminology and development of systems having common elements.

Emile Jaques-Dalcroze was an outstanding musician and an inspired teacher of music and movement whose work in eurhythmics is internationally famous. He was contemporary to Laban and many comparisons can be drawn between them. There were close links between them and they had mutual acquaintances. Suzanne Perrotet, Mary Wigman and Kurt Jooss were all pupils of Dalcroze and later were staunchly supportive of the view that gymnastics, movement, dance and creative expression form a syndrome of related ideas. They drew on each other's innovations, accepting some, rejecting others and gradually formulating recognizable systems.

After working as a professor at the Conservatoire in Geneva, Dalcroze went to Hellarau, near Dresden at the invitation of Wolf and Harald Dohrn where they built him a college for rhythmic training. At Hellarau, artistic pursuits were inaugurated which fired all Europe. Laban was an early visitor along with Stanislavsky, Wigman, George Bernard Shaw, Diaghileff and many others. A. S. Neill worked at Hellarau before returning to England to open Summerhill. Max Reinhardt, the revolutionary theatrical producer, with whom Laban was associated in Switzerland also visited Hellarau (Dutoit, 1970). Bienz, in correspondence tells of Laban's friendship with Max Reinhardt and the influence which the latter had on him, principally concerned with new art-forms applied to the theatre.

As with Laban, Dalcroze rejected his background and lived for a long time in an easy Bohemian fashion. Both men admired Isadora Duncan and there is evidence that Dalcroze influenced Laban directly in that, 'he (Laban) drew inspiration from the Hellarau Institute' (Dutoit 1970).

Susan Perrotet, Laban's mistress, was a Dalcroze pupil, and 'one of the first rhythmicians'. This has been advanced by Hall (1953) as an explanation for the Dalcroze influence attributed to Laban. Also, it can certainly be said that Dalcroze influenced Laban's close associate Jooss.

Dalcroze can be placed in the Platonic line. He re-discovered Plato's idea that 'the whole of man's life stands in the need of a right rhythm' (Sadler 1912). Dalcroze was influenced by Humboldt and Claparède whose writings were linked with the movement ideas of Laban through common concern with the powers of apperception and expression in the individual.

Dutoit (1970) put Dalcrose's first source of inspiration in Greece:

> though he was aware that Grétry, Gluck, Wagner, Schiller and Goethe had all tried before him to create an art analogous to that of Greek orchestic (Greek Dance).

The similarities of lineage between Dalcroze and Laban are further emphasized by Dutoit who puts Dalcroze firmly in the Delsarte /Noverre heritage.

In terms of this brief, Dalcroze is important because he was adventuring, at the same time, in a closely related field. There are many connections between the work of the two men. The Dalcroze work actually developed in England, in education, before Laban and acted as a platform from which Laban's work could develop. The man responsible for this was Percy Ingham. His contribution is discussed in detail later.

Certain similarities between Dalcroze and Laban have been noted but there were many differences. Dalcroze could be described as an élitist - he stressed improving those with talent; whereas Laban is more egalitarian, stressing Movement for all. The Dalcroze emphasis was on training hearing, while Laban emphasized kinaesthetics. There is less stress on rhythm alone in the work of Laban. Paddy Macmaster, a movement specialist trained by Leeder, believes that the Dalcroze system imposed more structure on the pupil. The music, for Dalcroze, suggests the movement, while for Laban the decision about movement involves taking other factors into consideration. Similarities are easier to find than differences. Dalcroze used similar terminology to Laban. He organized similar movement choirs. The festival at Lausanne in 1913 involved 1800 people. The fête de juin in 1914 at Geneva also involved a large movement choir. Dalcroze's 'plastique' concept is akin to Laban movement (Kennedy, 1950) and both require imaginative teachers for their systems. Both strove to link movement, music, intellectual activity and thought processes. Dalcroze comes very close to Laban in his ideas when he documents the aim of eurhythmy. He says that, 'it purifies the spirit, strengthens the will-power and instils order and clarity in the organism.'

Concerning Laban and Dalcroze, Mrs Tingey, President of the Dalcroze Teachers' Union has written:

> So far as Jaques' contact with Laban was concerned, both worked very amicably together at first in 1910 when Jaques went to Hellarau, but disagreed later in their respective views on the place of (a) music and movement and (b) dance and music.

Dalcroze stressed the 'eurhythmik' and Laban the 'eukinetik'.

The contribution of Percy Ingham to the development of Dalcroze's work in England is discussed fully in the *Journal of Scientific Physical Training* IV, II, 1912. Dalcroze's work was taken up early in this country mainly through the efforts of Ingham whose father had founded Moira House School, Eastbourne, in 1875 on startlingly modern lines; no marks, no prizes, no places in class. Art and music were integral parts of the curriculum, not extras! His aim was one education of the whole person and he was constantly on the alert for new methods to further his aim. In 1909 he had retired and his daughter had succeeded him, but he was still an active innovator. He contacted Jaques-Dalcroze in Geneva, saw the Dalcroze method as fulfilling a basic educational need and immediately arranged for it to be incorporated in the Moira House curriculum. Then he began to make it known in educational circles in England. At this point Jaques moved from Geneva to Hellerau, Dresden. Charles' daughter Gertrude, and his son, Percy, both went there for brief courses and were equally impressed by the value of the method. Percy decided to give up teaching and devote himself to its furtherance in England.

George Bernard Shaw visited Hellerau along with other English literary and artistic persons, principally because Ingham publicized the venture here.

Ingham interested many influential people in the work of Dalcroze. Sir W. H. Hadow, Vice Chancellor of Sheffield University wrote in glowing terms in an introduction to Dalcroze's book re-published in England in 1921. He stressed the aesthetic value of teaching self-expression through music and movement. In this, he is a very early advocate and publiciser of work which Laban was to take up later. Ingham's work helped to set the scene for a Laban approach later. He prepared the ground and attuned people to realizing that music and movement had educational significance. He enabled them to think about suitable clothing and the need to work in bare feet as well as weaning them away from Victorian ideas which prevented near-nude performances. Educational links between Dalcroze and Laban were still made in 1966. Keith Faulkner, Director of the Royal College of Music, wrote the introduction to yet another re-publication of Dalcroze's basic text. He emphasized the body as the child's first instrument – a concept common to both Laban and Dalcroze.

A liaison has always existed between the work of Dalcroze and Laban. Even when Laban came to England, Dalcroze pupils were here. Miss Edith Clark, one-time Staff Inspector of Physical Education, worked with Dalcroze and studied at Hellerau but also supported the efforts to introduce Laban movement in English schools. Currently, a course organized by the Dalcroze Society is led by a tutor from the Laban studio.

The work of Bode must be mentioned in an attempt to chart the ideological roots of Laban's work. Bode, a Dalcroze pupil created a system of rhythmical gymnastics using expressive techniques to promote natural movements. His basic principle of movement 'from the centre to the periphery' is an idea which is fundamental to many dance forms (Ross & Postma, 1954) and noted in Bodmer's synthesis of Laban's work. However, some of his ideas were bizarre. He thought that rhythmical gymnastics 'shaped the eye for beautiful movements'. Innovators such as Dalcroze, Bode, Laban and others of their genre occasionally became carried away with enthusiasm for an idea which, on reflection, appears trite and naive. The work of Bode has a genealogical significance. It paved the way for the work of his pupil, Heinrich Medau. The latter opened his school in Berlin in 1929. His system was particularly directed towards girls and women and stressed rhythmical flow and the dynamic qualities of movement. The system is concerned with 'an intimate relation between impulse and letting-go, tension and relaxation, the rise and fall characteristics of every Medau movement – a sort of pulsation'. In other words the polarity of Laban. Common characteristics stressed are wholeness and flow. Molly Braithwaite, President of the Medau Society in Great Britain acknowledges similarities between the ideas of Laban and Medau, and placed them as part of 'a wave of modern movement ideas which have come from Germany'. However, Medau and Laban never met (See Braithwaite, 1955). Prunella Stack, well-known in England as the founder of the 'Women's League of Health and Beauty', was a student of Medau. She considered his system superior to Laban's but in her autobiography, *Movement is Life,* gives no reasons for this. She associates the work of Laban and Medau but she is wrong when she says that Laban worked with Medau (Stack 1973).

Medau was born in Germany but lived for a long period in Portugal. He came to England in 1951 and worked in America. His work goes on in Germany today and the Medau Society still exists in England. The work failed to develop in England in the state system but is used in recreational classes. However, Medau movement existed in England before Laban. Peggy Secord introduced it before 1934 in extramural courses at Cambridge and on LEA courses organized by Essex at Dagenham. These continued spasmodically through until the 1940s. Medau performed the same type of 'John-the-Baptist' role with regard to Laban as Percy Ingham did for Dalcroze.

Medau has a further importance. He was ahead of his time in recommending the use of discovery methods. His other emphases were on 'relaxed waiting' and 'playing with pauses'. He tried to develop the rather bizarre concept of 'a gymnastics for the nerves'! Medau's work dovetails with Laban's contemporary work in the training of dancers in the 1930s in its stress on flow and the dynamic quality of movement. All these 'systems' appear sterile and stereotyped by today's standards. They are important in establishing links between the early study of movement and its applications to education. This was not done by Laban at the time but it is indicative of a background knowledge which was part of his heritage and which he used when he came to England.

Now enjoying something of a revival following Ken Russell's film, *Isadora,* Duncan was, in Laban's words, 'the mother of modern movement'. They were contemporaries and Laban (1948) is warm in her praise. A current assessment is that 'Duncan's place in the history of dance is assured – she was aware of Delsarte's work, met Dalcroze, and is acknowledged by Laban, Wigman and the American modern dancers as the founder of the new dance' (Layson, 1969). At interview, Ruth Foster, formerly HM Staff Inspector of Physical Education, said of Duncan, 'She made Laban possible.' Laban and Wigman may have based their dance systems on Duncan's theory of the gravitational principle of attraction and repulsion, tension and relaxation (Moore 1968). This is the polarity principle highlighted by Bodmer (1960) and discussed earlier. Bruce (1962) links the work of Duncan and Laban; the former 'without doubt influenced his thinking'. Both Laban and Duncan experienced a need to break away from the artificiality of dance as a stage art and saw it more as a central feature of life and living. Duncan's influence on Laban seems established 'without doubt'.

The links between Laban and Duncan are obvious, recognizable and well-researched. They had much in common in that they were both part of the mainstream of progressive thought current in the twenties. They represented a break-out from the frustration and resentment of the barren years of 1914–18 and epitomized the charisma of the Bohemian set. Their works show the attempts to link the artistic disciplines, to arrest interest by new approaches, and often to create 'artistic storms in aesthetic tea-pots' (Horst, 1968). Duncan had much in accord with the French impressionist and symbolic schools of painting and poetry, and in this was very close to Laban in her approaches to her art.

Laban was in Paris at the time of Isadora's first performance there in 1900. They were also later in Berlin at the same time. It is inconceivable that Laban would not have interested himself in her activities. One can only speculate on the extent of Duncan's influence on him but Laban in *Modern Educational Dance,* and *Principles of Dance and Movement Notation,* praises her and shows how she demonstrated successfully:

> . . . that there exists in the flow of man's movement some ordering principle which cannot be explained in the usual rationalistic manner.

Technical links between the art of Duncan and Laban do exist. What is more important is that Duncan achieved fame and publicity and partly prepared the way for Laban's later success. She made the new dance forms acceptable and re-awakened an interest in natural movement in laymen. She stressed the cathartic effects of expressive movement and she developed dance forms which fostered individual styles.

An artistic link between Laban and Oskar Schlemmer is suggested by Mauldon in Laban Guild Magazine articles in 1974/5. Schlemmer was a Bauhaus dancer and teacher who worked at this academy between about 1919 and 1930. Both Ullmann (See Laban 1935) and Mauldon document that Schlemmer worked with Laban and Wigman in 1927 at a dance congress where Pavlova was present. Schlemmer had links with Klee and Kandinsky and some connections with the Dada movement. He was interested in cosmic man and metaphysical issues – two very contemporary subjects of interest amongst those interested in the Arts at that time. Schlemmer also had very similar interests to Laban in his concern with Man and Geometry, and the relationship of mathematical theories to movement. There were differences in the thinking of the two men principally centring around the fact that Schlemmer had much more objectivity in his philosophy than did Laban. However, there is certainly a case for linking the two men artistically.

Architecture and freemasonry
At interview, Albrecht Knust was asked if he thought Laban was a religious man. He replied, 'He was probably not atheist'. Developing this theme, Knust said that Laban had been a freemason in Switzerland some time during the period 1910-20, and that it was this experience which had furthered his interest in architecture. Curl (1967a) also mentions this point. He says, 'Laban was very interested, and I believe he partook in Zurich in some of the mason's activities,' and later (Curl 1967b) 'But we know from Laban's Pythagorean, Sufism, Masonic and Mystic connections . . .' Sylvia Bodmer, one of Laban's oldest associates said during interview, 'Yes, he was a mason I know – he was a master – a grand master – he was a grand master that I know – he told us once – but he came from a catholic family you know – he went out again – you see he went out again because he didn't want to fix himself to such a particular ritual which was too limited.' Lisa Ullmann said he was a freemason between 1912-17. He left, she thought,

because of the political nature of freemasonry in Switzerland at that time as he, himself was 'non-political'. She thought he was 'high up' in the craft. Laban's daughter Juana had no knowledge of her father's freemasonry connections. Ullmann did not find this surprising. His children often write to her in the vein, 'What did my father think about . . .' The naivety of these replies is only seen when the truth about Laban's quasi-masonic activities as outlined in part one is known.

It was impossible for a long time to obtain verification of Laban's masonic activities. Masonic historians and the librarian at the archives of the United Grand Lodge of England were contacted and through them contact was made with an eminent mason living in Switzerland but there was no communication between the United Grand Lodge and the Alpine Order in Switzerland because of a dispute concerning masonic procedure. It was not possible to follow-up the inquiry at the time. Subsequently, correspondence was started, copies of which were received eventually, to try to locate someone who may have known Laban. After a great deal of searching contact was made with Mr Oscar Bienz, an Engineer now living in South Africa. Bienz was a source of great information. Copies of the principal correspondence are given in Appendix Two.

There are strong links between Laban's principles and masonic knowledge, skills and techniques which repay examination. According to Knust, Laban was fascinated by the masonic use of the golden rule. This idea, that perception naturally compares height with width in a given ratio was first noticed by Euclid in 3000 BC, and is used extensively in architecture to produce attractive form and strength. Artists of the Renaissance called it Divine Proportion. The Greeks used the Pentagon, which includes many divine proportion relationships as a holy symbol. The relationship, the longer element of which is approximately 1.618 times as long as the shorter (1.618 : 1), is also called the golden section, the golden ratio, the golden number, and the golden rule (Rowland, 1965). It is seen in paintings, human and animal forms and architecture. Perhaps the most obvious link between the golden rule concept and Laban's work is seen in his book on choreutics – the science dealing with the analysis and synthesis of movement (Laban, 1966). Choreutics is described by him as 'the practical study of the various forms of (more or less) harmonized movement'. In *Choreutics,* however, a study of both choreography and choreology (the logic and science of circles) is included under this title heading. The book was published eight years after his death and was assembled for publication by Lisa Ullmann who was assisted by Betty Redfern. Valerie Preston-Dunlop, an acknowledged expert, who reviewed the book (*LAMG Magazine No. 37, November 1966*) concluded 'I found it extremely heavy going'. She thought that it would probably be incomprehensible to students of movement and dance. This has been a constant criticism since that time. The reaons for this criticism may stem from the fact that Ullmann worked with a series of manuscripts containing original ideas which were unedited and un-polished. They were Laban's emerging, working ideas. When faced with presenting these ideas for publication, Ullmann tragically became bogged down in inadequately understood concepts and a welter of technical jargon where accepted, definitive meanings were not easily deduced.

One part of the book is based on the work of Gertrude Snell Friedburg which was completed in 1929. The other part was written about 1939. The emotional overtones expressed by Laban in the Preface and the relationship he implies between Choreutics and mysticism and supposed cosmic values are patently unacceptable to the majority of students today. This has devalued the work in the eyes of some people. In terms of content, choreutics is to Movement what key signatures are to music. It provides a scaffold for creative movement composition. One could question the validity of a use of choreutics at this time by the use of the music analogy. Music today has experimental approaches moving away from tonality and accepted forms. Is choreutics the most suitable vehicle for experimenting with movement structures today or do those on the frontiers of movement endeavours require a different blueprint?

Another serious criticism levelled at the interpretation of Laban's ideas in *Choreutics* is that after a fundamental use of icosohedral structures, Ullmann uses complex scales in basic cube forms. These are difficult for dancers to accept and have been hardly used in subsequent work in space harmony.

Choreutics as conceived by Laban was an original concept.

It was imaginative and inventive but it contained ideas which needed further study and deeper knowledge and use before they could conveniently be presented in print for the use of students. His presenters probably did the topic a disservice and held back the development of Laban's initial thinking by systematizing the work in text-book form at the time of publication. Also, the lack of practical suggestions about how the theoretical content could be used imaginatively has meant that the format as given has been used as a recipe when Laban would probably have preferred it to be a touch-paper which could be used to ignite more individual adventurous responses.

In the book, Laban (1966) shows something of the Golden Rule influence, although he does not acknowledge this specifically. He says:

> Movement is, so to speak, living architecture – living in the sense of changing emplacements as well as changing cohesion. This architecture is created by human movements and is made up of pathways tracing shapes in space, and these we may call 'trace-forms'. A building can hold together only if its parts have definite proportions which provide a certain balance in the midst of the continual vibrations and movements taking place in the material of which it is constructed . . . The living building of trace-forms which a moving body creates is bound to certain spatial relationships. Such relationships exist between the single parts of the sequence. Without a natural order within the sequence, movement becomes unreal and dream-like.

In this passage he implies the rather special relationship of the golden rule is at the root of human movement and draws an analogy between human movement and architectural strength. He writes that often, movement cannot be described by words only and in that case choreographic symbols are used. 'In this way, it is perhaps possible for space-movement to speak for itself.' Much of Laban's work is communicated more efficiently through symbols rather than words and a study of his diagrams shows that they contain the golden rule relationships on countless occasions as they illustrate movement. Perhaps a prime example is Laban's use of the icosahedron to illustrate space-orientation. The icosahedral scaffolding which he used to illustrate division of space through the moving body, sequential movement laws, and peripheral movements in space contains golden rule relationships throughout.

Laban considered the golden segment to be the ruling proportion between all the different parts of the perfectly built human body and throughout the ages its mathematical law has been linked with aesthetics. He generalizes from a knowledge of crystals (where the golden segment is seldom seen) to human behaviour. It appears that:

> The capacity to pack in a regular repeating space pattern is common among simpler substances which crystallize, but higher organisms do not exhibit this type of order (Curl, 1968).

In spite of this loose use of the golden rule which is acknowledged, the principle had real impact on Laban's fundamental ideas.

Laban was also influenced by masonic ideas of balance, equilibration and laws of forces. His ideas on 'Flow' contain the concepts of 'free flow' and 'bound flow'. In effort, he contrasts the gradations between 'fighting or contending' and 'indulging or yielding' attitudes in movement. His terminology draws on architectural and masonic principles but these are applied imaginatively to enable us to think in terms of movement rather than in terms of body mechanics.

Laban (1966) also draws on masonic plans. He writes:

> For our purpose, which is to find characteristic views offering a foundation for a multilateral description of movement, we may find it useful to select the following three aspects.
>
> 1 That of a mentality plunged into the intangible world of emotions and ideas.
>
> 2 That of the objective observer, from outside.
>
> 3 That of the person enjoying movement as bodily experience, and observing and explaining it from this angle.
>
> These three aspects can be taken as the three views – the ground-plan and the two views of elevation – on which we project the image of the object of our investigations: the unit, movement and space.

The use of plan and double elevation is an essential component of Laban's analysis and documentation of movement, and while he does not directly acknowledge his indebtedness to architectural and building science, concepts from these spheres

have been used to build up a model which he subsequently
applied to movement analysis.

Laban (1960) shows a great concern for the concepts of
Light and Darkness. It is a recurring idea with him. His basic
themes can be summed up in these quotations:

> The transformation of darkness into light, or of light into
> darkness is an elementary insight into the nature of our inner
> functions.

> In the inner light of acts of creation, the soul is reunited with the
> cosmic allness of space.

> One of the most interesting figures of speech is the concept of
> enlightenment which is the sudden understanding of something
> which has hitherto been hidden in the dark recesses of the mind.

In all these passages, there is the freemason's 'darkness visible'.
Part of the initiation ceremony in freemasonry is concerned
with the enlightenment into masonic knowledge to which
Laban refers. The initiate is released from a state of darkness
(being blindfolded) into masonic light. He discovers the three
great emblematical lights of freemasonry, the bible, the square
and compasses. Also the three lesser lights, the sun, the moon
and the master of the lodge. These are all used allegorically to
give masonic insights into the nature of 'the good life' in their
terms. Laban's ideas on light and darkness are not orignal. It is
likely that they owe something to masonry. Similarly Laban's
use of 'enlightenment' can be linked with the Gestalt view of
insight, an idea developed earlier. Freemasonry makes full and
rich use of analogy and symbolism, drawing on architectural
artefacts, and using these to illustrate principles of truth,
beauty, piety and goodness. Stress is laid on harmony, and the
pursuit of virtue. Laban used analogy to explain movement
concepts in architectural terms. He is also concerned 'to
discover the unity of movement'. A fact, 'that existed in ancient
times . . . and because it could not be explained, it assumed a
magic significance, and it is curious that even now it remains
magical, in spite of being analysed.' In this quotation, the
masonic idea of the mystical 'darkness visible' is evident again.
However, the stress on 'unity' could be explained in another
way. Laban's search for the key to the unity of movement has
already been shown to owe something to the work of the gestalt

school of psychologists working in Germany in the 1920s. Wertheimer and Koffka and their work would certainly be known to Laban. In his philosophies, he draws heavily on the idea of a 'gestalt', or an overall view of any particular movement action. The term 'movement' is often used as a gestalt to include the intellectual and physical components which go to make up a movement experience.

Scientific thought

Several German scientists originally studied ideas taken up in some detail by Laban. Friedrick Wilhelm Ostwald (1853–1932) was a physical chemist and a man of many-sided intellectual ability. He came to be regarded as an elder-statesman of physical chemistry, and indeed of science in general. He attached great importance to the concept of Energy, holding that the whole universe was a manifestation of energy in its various forms (Williams 1969). This concept can be likened to Laban's effort-rhythm which in one book (Laban & Lawrence, 1947) he sees as the cohesive medium of much of man's achievements, and the basis of movement and behaviour in everyday life. In the same way Laban often sees movement as synonymous with energy and refers to it, in terms of basic motivation as 'an independent power creating states of mind frequently stronger than man's will' (Laban, 1948).

Ernst Mach formulated a theory that knowledge was a matter of sensation (Asimov, 1966). Furthermore, he was against the notion that space and time were anything more than generalizations built up from observation. The properties of space had no independent existence but were dependent on the mass content and distribution within it. Moreover, what we call time was merely the comparison of one set of movements with a standardized movement (that of the hands of a clock for instance). This view of time and space is very much in the Laban mode. Mach's ideas on the properties of space coincide closely with Laban's. The latter saw all man's movement organized into a general space sphere. The places he strives towards arise out of his physiological-psychological structure and are the focus of his own attempts at equilibrium – the interaction between man and space suggested by Mach. Did Laban glean any ideas from Mach? This is an academic question – but the connection between the thinking is there. No doubt, there are movement theorists who would wish to support and attack the thesis.

The work of Ernst Heinrich Weber merits consideration. He found that the minimum difference in intensity that could be distinguished between two sensations of identical kind bore a constant relationship to the total intensity of sensation. For instance, suppose a person could distinguish between a nine ounce weight and a ten ounce weight. This would seem to indicate that he could therefore distinguish between a 90 ounce weight and a 91 ounce weight. This is not so. He will be able to distinguish only between a 90 ounce weight and a 100 ounce weight. It is not a difference on one gram or ten grams that is important but the difference of 10% of the total weight (Asimov, 1966). In the same way, in telling the difference between intensities of light or sound, differences in temperature or pressure, it is the percentage difference which counts. This is the Weber-Fechner law. Its importance here is that its popularization in Germany, following Fechner's work, was considerable and would have been available to Laban. The law forms the basis for all kinds of experimentation into the manner in which the human-being senses the environment about him, and how he interprets his sense impressions. What part does movement play in the latter? Are the main control variables cognitive, affective or motor? These questions are still unanswered but researches into the problem would use the work of Laban and the scientists mentioned here. The aim here is two-fold. First to hypothesize the possible link with Laban's work and second to open up a new area of thought which would draw on Laban's theories.

In summary, no logical tap-root emerges from a study of the influences on Laban. There are many strands which are linked with his work. This is not unusual. In an attempt to regularize a set of principles governing a predominently creative activity, the patterns of thinking are likely to be more open-ended than step by step logical progressions. The power-house or drawing-force behind his thinking is not a unitary influence but a complex series of experiences. Similarly, the derivatives from these sources appear to be equally diverse. They concern many disciplines but in a haphazard, sometimes almost slipshod, manner.

LABAN AND
ENGLISH EDUCATION

Movement Education in Schools

Introduction

The Laban art of movement can be seen in education, industry, therapy, theatre and recreation (Redfern, 1965). There is, however, a definite educative aspect in all the areas mentioned as well as in Education specifically. The use of Laban's ideas has influenced training in industry; the preparation of therapists and the therapy they practise; the theatre schools who train professional actors and the content and methods of their courses; and recreation, leisure and the keep-fit movement.

Laban was not a physical educationist and yet his work has revolutionized this discipline. His theories have received official support from the Department of Education and Science and the former Ministry of Education through the organisation of in-service courses to further the use of his principles in schools. The Laban Art of Movement Studio Course is recognized as a suitable training which leads to qualified teacher status:

> Courses at the Studio have been linked with those offered at Trent Park College of Education to lead to qualified teacher status. In 1973, arrangement has been made for the Studio to be taken over completely from the present trustees by the administration authorities of Goldsmiths' College, London. Thus the Movement Department of this college and the Studio are now integrally linked under one Principal, Miss Marion North.

Local authorities such as London (LCC, 1963) and the West Riding have published books geared to the needs of serving teachers and based on Laban's principles. Thus, they have given official backing to the development of these ideas in schools.

It is not surprising that Laban could make such an impact from his atypical background. A large proportion of innovators in the field of education and teaching have not been professional educationists:

> Comenius worked in and organised schools but he was a theologian and philosopher. Rousseau never held classes and had a strange history of unconcern with regard to his own children. Froebel was a chemist and philospher, Herbert a psychologist and philosopher, Montessori, Décroly and Claperède were doctors of medicine and the latter two were also psychologists. Dewey was a philosopher, and more latterly, Piaget is a zoologist turned genetic epistomologist. Also in recent times, real impact on education has been made by sociologists, neuro-physiologists, linguists and paediatricians. Piaget himself has studied this phenomenon and asks the question, 'Is the reason inherent in the nature of pedagogy itself, in the sense that its lacunae are a direct effect of the impossibility of achieving a stable equilibrium between its scientific data and its social applications?' He concludes, 'The truth is that the profession of education has not yet attained in our societies' (Piaget 1971). In physical education and other disciplines, the literature is often first written by laymen. Guts-Muths was a geographer, Veth a teacher of mathematics, Jahn and Ling were philologists and Laban was an eclectic whose interests centred on a variety of arts.

What was important about Laban, a newcomer to English Physical Education, was that he had influential contacts who were able to present his ideas to teachers; namely, many of the physical educationists who were interviewed in connection with this publication. Before these people could work, they had to be trained and begin to apply Laban's ideas to Education. The practical application of these ideas in England was first developed by Lisa Ullmann. As Principal of the Laban Art of Movement Studio, she was the person who became the first power-house of transmission in turning a set of poorly formed hypotheses into a workable classification capable of educational interpretation. Leonard Elmhirst writes 'If there had been no Lisa, there would have been very little left of Laban.' However, he does show her limitations also when he says, 'Lisa's trouble was the strict limitations of her own horizon so that her technique was way ahead of her capacity to use it in an artistically meaningful way.'

In the implementation of any new ideas, some of them are misunderstood, badly interpreted and often misused. At times 'disciples' over-systematize ideas. The Laban movement has been aware of this . . . ('He wanted people not to have 'Laban Movement' but the experience of the whole world of movement and he handed out tools to make this experience richer' (Ullmann)) but often has done little to deter systems as they have arisen, and although Ullmann says 'I find excessive talk of Rudolph Laban's analysis of movement rather frightening', the Guild appears to invoke a fanatical following of Laban's theories more than their imaginative development. For example, there is a remarkable sameness about Guild articles. Too many are personal statements, introspective, ingenuous accounts of the writers' own Damascus road experiences. Far too many others are eulogies . . .

> We owe Mr Laban a great deal for the deeper meaning he has brought into our lives, but when we try to commit to paper what we have learned from him we do not do him justice (Sherborne LAMG Magazine No. 2, Nov. 1964).

> When Mr Laban and Miss Ullmann were teaching there . . . Who could resist such nectar. (Secretary's report LAMG Magazine No. 6).

> This year the lecture . . . was a biographical talk on Rudolph Laban . . . it was a foretaste of pleasures to come, a book about Mr Laban. (LAMG Magazine No. 30, 1963). The book is still not written!

> At every dance lesson, I wore my dance tunic . . . which being a vivid purple was duly admired (LAMG Magazine No. 25, 1958).

In 1950, five pages were devoted to 'The birthday party' and an account of musical arms! ('Miss Ullmann succeeded in outwitting everyone and winning the event with sustained quickness'). Another heading was 'Some anecdotes about Mr Laban'. Knowing his background as detailed earlier, his wry sense of humour may well have been stimulated by the trivia which followed! It is this atmosphere which is so much in contrast to Laban's previous background in the arts. His Bohemian outlook is now replaced by an ultra-confirmist, schoolmistress circle. A study of the Guild magazine through the years and indeed as late as 1974 shows a preoccupation with looking back and searching for more anecdotes about Laban. This must be considered inappropriate in the midst of the most fundamental educational changes ever encountered.

The Laban causerie could not have dreamed in the early days of the nation-wide use of his work in the future. At that time, they were a tightly-knit, small body with the characteristics of an extended family, enjoying the patronage of the patriarchal figure of Laban. Their sphere of interest was more in human movement for its own sake than its educational uses. In 1954 Laban wrote a letter to all Guild members. An analysis of this reveals that he covered these ten topics:

> Aetiology of body defects
> Effects of movement training on bed-ridden patients
> Psychological effects of the art of movement
> Social welfare
> Working efficiency in industry
> Personal adjustment and the art of movement
> Theatrical performance
> Harmony of movement
> Morphology (sciénce of forms in nature) and movement
> Notation (LAMG Magazine, No. 137 1954)

None of these is specifically aimed at education. In keeping with his early work, he is still dance and movement geared. Excerpts from 'Der Narrenspiegal' (Laban, 1920a) were published in the Guild magazine in October 1955. This extract shows no educational content and indeed, the comment in the article does not make any at that time. As late as 1961, Dewey (1961), in examining the significance of Laban's studies in human movement is wholly taken up with the art and science of the study. Even by one of Her Majesty's Inspectors there is little application to schools.

The early years were movement-centred. Imaginative work was developing in schools but only in isolated pockets, spurred on by workers like Diana Jordan, Ruth Foster, Margaret Dunn, Elsie Palmer and Myfanwy Dewey working mainly in

Lancashire and Yorkshire. In retrospect, this was probably inevitable. These were ground-work years when future pioneers and trainers were being schooled themselves. The movement at this time was implosive. The explosive phase was to follow.

Pre-Laban

It is possible to trace a form of movement education throughout the history of the growth of physical education. It is axiomatic that in the development of the games tradition and the evolution of the various gymnastic systems, movement education was a component part. It is outside the brief of this study to indicate such relationships. The aim here is to focus on dance-centred movement education which was apparent pre-Laban which had some of the elements seen in Laban's work.

The Swedish system, following the ideas of Ling gained ground from 1878 onwards. At this time Mathias Roth and Alice Westlake were instrumental in persuading the London School Board to appoint Corcordia Lofving as Lady Superintendent of Physical Education. Corcordia Lofving influenced Martina Bergmann and when the latter founded what is now known as Dartford College, she was receptive to new ideas concerned with movement education. At Dartford, Bedford and Anstey Colleges, from the turn of the century, work concerning kinaesthetics and eurhythmics was closely examined and tried experimentally. Naturally, their main work was concerned with Swedish gymnastics but an important point is that they were receptive to new ideas and reflective about them. Woman physical educationists were closely connected with emancipation. Mary Hankinson, a founder of the Ling Association was a suffragette. The women's colleges often saw new ideas and approaches as an opportunity to assert the independence of women. Any activities which helped this ideal were studied.

The eurhythmics of Jaques-Dalcroze were practised in England from about 1912. They were preceded by the new gymnastics for families and schools associated with Dio Lewis and Moses Coit Tyler. These new gymnastics had a eurhythmic element in them and appealed to people interested in less stereotyped movement. Dalcroze's work flourished, led by the propaganda and influence of Percy Ingham. By 1920, over

2,800 pupils had undertaken courses in Eurhythmics in this country and most of these went to run courses for others. The eurhythmic movement entered the curriculum of progressive private schools and became a recreative activity for women in clubs and at health centres. Johnstone (1924) writes of the observations she made of Dalcroze classes in Manchester Schools. She was impressed by much of what she saw but often found the work too directed. She concluded, 'The fault lies with the system, not the teacher.' She did not see eurhythmics taking the place of 'physical training' but supporting it, and even in 1922 she asked the question, 'What generalized influence does it have on mind and body?' Perceptively and predictively she comments that its best effects were with 7-12 year olds, and that it failed with older boys – 'The whole matter seems to bore them.' The Dalcroze system at this time, received full support from Miss Edith Clarke when she was Staff Inspector of Physical Education. She has recently written about this and referred to 'the beautiful movement, achieved through rhythm and natural movement' brought about by Dalcroze training (Clarke, 1972).

Clarke's use of the term 'natural movement' is very much of her generation. Some schools were experimenting with natural movement as part of their curriculum, no doubt influenced by the publicity received by Isadora Duncan. Madge Atkinson was one of the foremost pioneers. She was influenced by Aimie Spong, a Duncan pupil. Atkinson was a forerunner of Laban and identified by him as such. She worked extensively in Manchester in the early 1920s and was influenced by the philosophies of Rudolph Steiner (Kennedy 1950). Her basic guideline was that the germ of rhythmic action lay within the child and only needed appropriate stimuli for it to develop. 'The heart of Miss Atkinson's ideal is the old Greek ideal – the intrinsic unity of movement and music' – an idea which has much in common with Laban. Atkinson focused attention on movement timing, speed and flow. She was concerned with quality of effort and both functional and expressive movement. Her terminology is dated. She frequently talks about primitive instincts, but this is entirely natural at the time of McDougall. She had links with Manchester Training Colleges and her students were interested in introducing natural movement in elementary schools (Johnstone, 1924).

Another movement teacher was Diana Watts who also worked in the North West in the 1920s. Watts was an American dancer. She published her philosophy of movement in 1914. This was based on a thorough study of classical Greek statues and paintings of the archer, the discus thrower and the runner. She emphasized tension and relaxation, balance and elasticity of movement, and linked all these with ability to concentrate. Her approach foreshadowed Laban in the applications of mathematics to human movement which she made. Her work was also in the Gurdjieff tradition which was associated with Laban's thinking (Sweeney, 1970).

Margaret Morris was another movement pioneer. She opened her own school in 1910 offering a complete stage training which linked movement with the creative arts. She was a pupil of Raymond, brother of Isadora Duncan and was romantically attached to John Galsworthy who encouraged her. She eventually married J. D. Fergusson, the Scots painter. She tried repeatedly until World War II 'to get free movement given a try-out in Council Schools' but with no success (Morris 1969). She writes that she is delighted that at last it is being used, 'though it could only be accepted from a foreign country' – a reference to the success of the Laban work. Her work and the publicity she attracted prepared the ground for Laban and helped to create a climate where the inception of his ideas was possible.

Laban acknowledged her contribution in his own genealogical table of modern dance. Significantly, she thought the physical education colleges were very reactionary (although I have shown that they could be receptive to new ideas) and reports on a visit to Dartford . . . 'Every time the arms came sharply to the sides, there was a loud cracking of starched sleeves.' She is similarly critical of Chelsea College who were politely appreciative but unreceptive to the idea of natural movement in the college. Morris' work is, however, rooted in her own era. Her latest book gives 'What every Margaret Morris teacher should know', in question and answer form! She was a pioneer though and unknown to Laban produced an embryo system of notation in 1928, the year that Laban published his book *Schrifttanz* in Germany.

The BBC had taken up the interest in eurhythmics and before Laban's work had made any national impact, Ann

Driver, a trained Dalcroze teacher, was a popular radio figure with her *Music and Movement* programmes for both children and adults. Ruby Ginna had similar ideas to Morris and Atkinson. She opened a school of 'revived Greek dancing' known as the Ginna Mawr School which operated in Boscastle, Cornwall with an approach akin to the natural movement of Atkinson. She trained Anita Hayworth who, until 1973 was operating the London School of Dance, working on the principles of natural movement. Laban produced a genealogical table of modern dance and gave this to a course held at Moreton Hall from 31 December 1941-6 January 1942. In this, he noted the contribution of Morris, Ginna and Atkinson who represented the current and immediate past dance scene in England at that time. The use which Laban made of the 'pre-Laban scene' is well illustrated by this same course which was advertised in the Times Educational Supplement as concerned with showing how the Central European influences (Laban's dance) could be linked with dance based on natural movement.

Before Laban's work had made much headway, Maja Carlquist visited England. Her work, based on Ling's principles, was shown extensively here in 1946. It had more in common with the 1933 Syllabus than 'Moving and Growing' but it indicates interest in movement education stemming from other sources besides Laban in the 1940s which established an atmosphere where development could take place.

The ethos which 'allowed Laban to happen' had built up gradually and imperceptibly since the turn of the century. The fillip given to physical education generally by the revelations concerning health revealed by recruits for the Boer War is well-known. Similarly the Report of the Royal Commission on Physical Training (Scotland) in 1903, and the Report of the Interdepartmental Committee on Physical Deterioration in 1904 had their effects. Volume II of a series of special enquiries on education subjects (begun by the Education Department in 1894) had highlighted Physical Education and promoted the cause of Swedish gymnastics. The appointment of Sir George Newman to the Ministry in 1907 was important. He made quick progress to develop physical education by appointing four inspectors in 1908. They were Captain Grenfell, Dr Heald, Miss Koetter and Miss Palmer (both the latter from Dartford College). Francis Henry Grenfell (1874–1945) was truly a contemporary of Laban. He developed physical education in schools widely. An ex-navy man, he saw physical education answering many of the social needs of the time. These needs grew out of the Boer War and the 1914–18 war, and rapid industrial expansion followed by recessions, unemployment and strikes. His approach had little in common with Laban but nevertheless he 'popularized' physical education, and made it a vital part of the curriculum. Once this had been done, change, in the form of Laban movement was possible.

Earlier development had been accepted because of social need. Laban's work received acceptance because it was essentially an individual approach at a time, after World War II, when individual differences were being stressed. It was expressive at a time when self-expression was becoming fashionable, and it was a non-academic outlet when widening concepts of intelligence were leading educationists to look for creative outlets for non-academic pupils.

Curriculum

Lisa Ullmann was the main motivating force in taking Laban into the educational orbit. A practical reason for this was that they needed the money which educational courses provided. However, Ullmann's inexperience as an educationist is very obvious. She was readily in print, often bogged down in broad generalizations and inadequately understood half-truths. Her early writings show no awareness of the complex problems faced by teachers in English schools as they attempted to introduce Movement into their work. She knew 'Movement' but could not help teachers to use the knowledge she gave them to enrich their work in its entirety. The origins of Movement as a watertight compartment on the periphery of the curriculum are undoubtedly here. The language presented a problem to her and Laban. She wrote in cliché terms about 'Movement as a basis for living'. It is obvious that she could know little of the more rigorous approaches to curriculum planning which were beginning to develop at that time but her early work did invite severe criticism because of its vagueness and ingenuousness. A study of the Guild magazine up to 1967 fails to reveal any rigorous examination of the place of movement education in the curriculum in anything but the most vague terms. 'Movement is a fundamental phenomenon of life' is a central theme, usually accompanied by the Froebelian concept of 'inter-relationships of inner attitudes and outer-bodily de- meanours (Ullmann, 1960). There is little attempt to define objectives, specify learning experiences designed to achieve these, and indicate forms of evaluation. Perhaps at that time, this was an essentially American pastime, but it has become 'de rigeur' in the English literature subsequently. It could have been done as early as 1960. Diane Gaumer, writing in the Laban Guild magazine in that year clearly points the way with quite the most penetrating, perceptive article on the art of movement in Education presented at that time or for many succeeding years. She built a systematic case for the inclusion of Movement in the curriculum and discussed these factors:

> The aims and values of the art of movement.
> What are the principles of creative teaching?
> Aims and values, and their links to current ideas in schools.
> The role of movement education in a changing society.
> The examination of dance as part of the curriculum.
> The teacher/pupil relationships and how movement education enhances this.
> A discussion of lesson plans.
> Check lists used for evaluation.
> The use of demonstration and production.
> Movement education – an approach via the arts and/or physical education.
> Movement and development (Gaumer 1960).

Many of these issues are still apparent and unresolved. The list given could serve as an outline for a publication which would have wide appeal today. Gaumer pointed the way forward and indicated the problems to be faced in 1960. There is little evidence that they were taken up with any stringency or intellectual vigour for many years. The devotees were still concerned with the mystic metaphysics and a certain divine rightness of their subject. Objective opinion from informed specialists was available though. One of the more positive views was that:

> This work of Mr Laban may well prove to be even more important than that of Ling, since it is concerned with the

aesthetic and creative possibilities of movement, while at the same time, its analysis is detailed and exact (Whiting, 1956).

This point of view indicates the possibility for development and the problems to be faced but it was largely ignored and the somewhat artless approach continued.

Contemporary issues are mostly foreshadowed in the 1950s. Ann Hutchinson (1956) suggested teaching Laban's notation in schools at a very early age:

> The basic elements of movement can be explored at the age of four or five, and at this time, the symbols representing these should be introduced. Even if they never use the notation later on, they will have gained from having studied it. For many this valuable tool turns out to be a key, a key to open up new doors in movement education and understanding.

Do we teach notation? This is a controversial question. It still exercises physical educationists and divides them. Sixteen years after this article, no research evidence is available on its impact, value and viability as an aspect of the curriculum. In 1973, some progress has been made. A Notation Research Project has been financed based at Anstey College of Physical Education with £3,000 per annum for three years to examine the possibilities of notation usages in Education and Industry and possibly the theatre.

In examining method, an important dichotomy can be discerned even in the early days. The first experimental work in movement education was centred in Lancashire and Yorkshire. This was because the Laban Art of Movement Studio was first opened in Manchester and so had close contact with Lancashire schools, and also because liaison was soon established between the studio and the advisers and teachers of the West Riding authority under the direction of their very sympathetic education officer, Sir Alec Clegg. Movement education developed in two distinct ways on each side of the Pennines. In Lancashire, the accent was on free experimentation and development stemming initially from children's natural movements. The structure of movement was built on afterwards. In Yorkshire, the vocabulary of movement, much of it couched in Laban's own terms, was taught in an imaginative but somewhat formal manner. Basic movement skills concerned with expressive movement were taught as exercises and a degree of proficiency was obtained in these. This was considered an important starting point and an end in itself. The creative use of these movements and their natural development as an aid to expression, emotional release, and individual fulfillment came after the movement vocabulary had been acquired. There is a case for both these approaches. Indeed, it is invidious to suggest one correct mode of operation. An eclectic approach using both techniques has developed since and even this will alter as more is learned about modes of thinking in children, and identification of individual cognitive style. In the early days, however, positions in Lancashire and Yorkshire became somewhat polarized. Each side thought they had the answer to methodology. Leonard Elmhirst concludes 'Without a doubt, the West Riding made the most creative use of Laban's work and attracted original minds in the world of Movement.' This is probably true. The Lancashire work eventually became centred in the Manchester Dance Circle whose interests ranged much wider than purely schools work. Sir Alec Clegg also identified the dichotomy (Ward, 1951). He is quoted as saying that there were two conflicting theories in the presentation of movement training, and that these also showed in the teaching of other subjects, notably Art. The one theory was concerned with teaching a technique, the other aimed at keeping alive the joy of creating and retaining the love of beauty so often blunted or killed by less sensitive teaching. Elma Casson and Margaret Dunn, both formerly concerned with the organization of movement education in the West Riding were aware of this difference in method and attributed it to the influence of Elsie Palmer in Lancashire. However, they did not see one approach as right and the other as wrong but as two approaches to a difficult question of method. Clegg talks about 'conflicting theories' but this is not an apt description. The theories were more complementary than conflicting and show the possibilities for innovative, original use of a common idea.

The two approaches have been systematized further over the years. The early work has been moulded into a series of patterns. The success which these schemes have enjoyed has been their weakness. Success has been repeated; a formula has been established, and the result, after two decades has sometimes been an inflexible system, easily recognized as movement from a certain area or even a particular school. This is a factor which has opened up movement to criticism from truly progressive educators. North (1964a) rightly deprecates inflexibility – 'There will, therefore be no stereotyped forms' (of movement). She hopes that if students and teachers really understand principles, they can and must justify creative deviation and have this accepted by authorities. Wise counsel in 1964 and still a necessary crie-de-coeur today. Physical education students abhor the fact that they are given too much chapter and verse; taught a recognizable end-product, and not allowed more individual interpretations. Although this position still exists today, there are many voices against it. The problem and its cause is identified in the statement:

> The basic movement themes which Laban put forward are not worded in analytical terms. What analysis has been done in this field has been done by a second generation of practitioners, working on Laban's syntheses (Preston-Dunlop, 1967a, 1967b).

It is in the colleges of education where the analysis has been made and the structure put on Laban's network of thoughts. When this has happened, some students, with less than a full insight into his work, have gone into schools and copied and replicated the college model. This happened in general training for primary teaching where demonstration classrooms existed in colleges. These were slavishly built up by students in their schools and often were quite unsuitable for the children who used them and the buildings where they were housed.

Although Laban's theories have become the basis of schemes of physical education and have replaced to a large extent, in women's work especially, the anatomical and physiological approach which existed previously, he had no impact on the modern dance movement in England which was never strong (Lester, 1961). In fact, the visit of Martha Graham and her company from the USA in 1954 'was a significant introduction to Britain of a unique dance form'. Similarly, Laban had little or no impact on either the American modern dance scene or the work of movement in education (Wooten, 1957; Shawn, 1946). Laban's influence, at this time, became education-centred. His impact on the dance world became less direct.

The place of physical education in inter-disciplinary

enquiry and integrated schemes, the use of flexible groupings, free-choice activities, and team-teaching are all current issues of curriculum controversy.

The debates concerning these issues have occurred during the last few years. They are not completely contemporary though. Work of over twenty years ago foreshadowed debate still existing today. In 1960, attention was drawn to the need for opening up the concept of Movement and taking it out of narrow confines:

> The analysis (of Laban) permits a generalized mode of thought which is extremely fruitful; it opens up infinite possibility in the world of movement, and within these ultimate conceptions of Space, Time, Energy, both the more particular descriptions, such as those of actions in games, and the more mixed, such as rhythm and momentum, have perspective (Foster, 1960).

This article demonstrated the integrating character of Movement Study and showed that Laban's principles permitted both analysis and synthesis. These ideas from 1960 link closely with work on individual cognitive style much later. Satterley and Brimer (1971) have suggested modes of thinking which they divide into analytic and synthetic, categories which have much in common with convergent and divergent thinking styles suggested by many psychologists today. This element in Laban's analysis shows that his bases can be used for imaginative development by pupils who have a wide variety of cognitive styles. Also, the appeal of the principles as a vehicle for many different modes of thinking is an element of confirmation of how it caters for the individual, and that it is a basic integrator in human behaviour. The opportunity which Movement can give to exercise a range of different cognitive styles is a valuable asset. In this subject, there is a need for further research.

The problem of ensuring increased flexibility, and linking Movement with other subjects, especially the creative arts has appeared in the literature for many years but the educational principle of integration and use of the movement lesson to heighten other experiences in the arts was seldom suggested. Rather, integration was hinted at in general terms, and the idea of a fusion of interests was confined to a joint-arts concept. Throughout the sixties, however, there was growing awareness of the need to integrate movement with other aspects of the curriculum. In 1967, Percival wrote as headmaster of a well-known grammar school:

> I have seen enough of the best work done in educational gymnastics and modern dance to be certain that here is an activity that can not only bring deep aesthetic and emotional experiences but also help to develop a sense of poise and personal identity. Why should not this range of work spill over into courses in good grooming, developing clothes sense, all types of dancing, the art of entertaining, good speech and manners, drama, music and art activities? And be done by the same people! In some ways, there may be more links between these courses and dance, than between that and the traditional coaching of games.

This embryonic view of inter-disciplinary enquiry was also seen in the Newsom report which stressed the central role of the art of movement for girls and saw it enhancing their concern with fashionable good looks and their eventual adult interests.

The case against specialist physical education colleges working as 'monotechnics' is often made. In any inter-disciplinary courses, physical education should figure strongly but physical education teachers are often ill-prepared for this approach. Training in a multi-purpose college may help the problem. In the post-James era, it is a view shared by many, but the James Report itself suggested physical education as an area where the monotechnic element may still be appropriate! This is another unresolved issue. Laban's early work suggests some kind of integrated approach to Movement; but this could emerge from a specialist college providing that a new ethos was assumed by the college. Physical Education in the 1980s will demand completely changed ideas from the legacies of the post-war years. The likelihood is that a variety of systems will emerge. Physical education and the training of physical education teachers will undoubtedly take place in multi-purpose colleges, especially where existing facilities in large colleges are suitable for this. Where this happens, it is likely that Laban principles will form part of the curriculum. The new image of the specialist physical education college, which still remains a possibility through the James committee proposals, is at the formative level. Colleges which may assume this role are examining their possible structure. Ideas for consideration include sports resources centres, the whole spectrum of the recreation and leisure industries, movement consultancies, human movement specialisms, outdoor education centres and counselling work. In all these ideas, there are possibilities for training aides, auxiliaries, coaches and instructors alongside more professional categories. There is also a developing role for therapy, and an awareness that the new ethos must be radically changed from that which characterized the institutions formerly. Whereas before, the colleges provided courses 'to study the theory and practice of movement based on Laban's principles and the application of these principles to all aspects of physical activity included in the College curriculum', in the future this concept may be widened to achieve a more eclectic approach. Laban's influence will not be diminished but it will not be the sole raison d'être; rather a major contributor to a more pan-disciplinary approach to the study of movement.

There is much talk about integration today but few accounts of it in practice. How to accomplish it successfully presents problems which will only be solved by school-based empiricism. The need is for a system which allows pupils to follow self-initiated enquiry and then use movement to help solve the problems they meet. Such systems are developing in the Middle Schools and have been apparent in Primary Schools for some time now. In another study, many schemes which use movement in this way have been described (Foster, 1972a). One example may serve as illustration here. A group of junior children had been studying St. Paul's journeys. They were discussing the problem of rejection at one port of call. At this point, the teacher took them into the hall and worked out a movement theme to help them to experience the feelings and relationships which existed at this port. Afterwards, they returned to the classroom to continue their expressive work which showed a new awareness of many parts of the story. The movement had been used at the core of the study, to help in the creative work the children were doing. It was seen to have relevance and value, and its importance was significantly more than purely physical exercise.

The example shows the use of discovery learning in Movement Studies which is intricately bound up with integrated approaches; the latter is achieved most often through the use of the former. Weiner and Lidstone (1969) link Movement and discovery learning approaches and state a case which is illustrated by the example used. They say:

> Perhaps the greatest contribution that creative dance can make to the classroom is to re-introduce the kind of experimental learning that goes on at the pre-school level, where the child participates in explorative, non-judgmental activities with real things. The child in creative movement has an opportunity to re-discover the self through thoughts and feelings – to know again that the self originates nowhere but in himself, in his own body, his own movement, his own sensations.

The central role of movement in the formation of concepts is implicit in this statement which also shows how the activity can be used as part of the child's exploratory behaviour. A recent symposium on movement education in America (Sweeney, 1970) has many contributions drawing on research in discovery learning and the acquisition of skill. These readings establish links between creative response and movement. Problem-solving, exploration and the use of movement as a way of learning are all discussed. All these approaches would give movement education a more central place in the curriculum.

Armytage (1972) links discovery learning and an integrated approach in the training of physical education teachers. He suggests the writing of personal autobiographies and the introspective analysis of induced problems. 'Such a loosening of the tongue liberates a force that can arouse drives, mediate rewards and facilitate ongoing activity in learning, problem-solving or planning. Once that tongue can fashion verbal labels then its owner can perceive, discriminate, and make those mental trial and error judgements so important in any learning situation.' Students need to have experienced discovery learning and integrated approaches if they are to use them successfully with their pupils. Integration and discovery learning can be included in many of the skills activities forming part of the normal physical education curriculum. The individualization of circuit-training, the use of pro-grammed learning in the theoretical and practical elements of skill acquisition, and the use of individual assignments to work out space-harmony problems are all examples of these approaches.

There are many strands to the curriculum development process in physical education. These concern practical and academic development, changing content leading to new methods and techniques of operation, and the effects of the previous issues on the role and status of those concerned with physical education. The split between physical education and movement studies is again apparent, and the philosophical debates concerning the aims and objectives of the subject are also raised. The influence of Laban's work touches every branch of these debates in some way, and this is the particular interest and focal point of the comment made in this study.

In the Dance sector, Preston-Dunlop has been concerned with further creative development of Laban's work. She showed at interview and in her published work that she was dissatisfied with the status-quo. Now she sees the need for impetus from outside the traditional Laban circle to enliven his work, and stresses the necessity of linking movement with things which can be done outside school, particularly in leisure activites. One suggestion she made is for the use of Martha Graham's movement in a developmental growth from Laban's Modern Educational Dance. This could be restricting and less creative on the one hand, but a good teaching tool on the other hand. She rejects the Graham method but uses the content to build on Laban's work. There is a principle here. Preston-Dunlop is prepared to examine Laban's work afresh, to articulate it in new settings, and to use the ideas of others to clothe the body of basic ideas he formulated. This principle is central to curriculum development if any real deviations are to be made and growth is to take place.

An uncomfortable relationship exists between physical education and human movement studies:

> Although professional aspects of physical education have received great attention, the body of knowledge fundamental to a study of human movement has not been developed (Corlett & Webb, 1971).

There has been too much concern with the purpose of education rather than the field of study. Empirical inquiry has only recently begun to look at human movement in its own right. How will these two facets be linked in the future? Human movement or a wider concept of movement studies will emerge as an academic field of study. If this happens, the influence of Laban may be considerable. He has provided a framework of codified knowledge which is essential to the students of this emerging discipline. Academic work within this confine at the secondary or higher education level will contain a large element of study concerned with Laban's principles and other movement concepts.

Warren Lamb (1964) writes as a movement consultant outside education. He supports the view of Movement as a subject outside the traditional concept of Physical Education and believes that:

> The more that the Art of Movement becomes irrevocably linked with the teaching profession, and recognized as a method of teaching, the more unlikely it is that it will ever exist as a basic discipline.

In the future, academic inquiry will centre around 'Human Movement Studies'. There are implications in this for examinations and the content of studies in higher education. At school level many curricula problems remain - What to teach, to whom and how! The tools to make these decisions exist in the new theoretical approaches to curriculum planning. The work has begun but much remains to be accomplished.

In the thinking which characterizes teacher-education today, there is implication for curriculum change in schools. As teacher-education changes and students leave colleges with new skills and knowledge, so they take parts of their interests into schools and gradually these appear in the curriculum. If a new, wider concept of the specialist physical education college emerges, graduate and undergraduate work will be undertaken. Dance therapists, research scholars in movement, artist teachers, artist performers, and ethnic dance authorities are some of the categories of professional who may be produced by the change in style of the colleges (Hawkins, 1967). If this happens, all these groups would influence school work directly or indirectly and assist curriculum change. They, through their training would probably be influenced by Laban's ideas.

Will a movement approach to teaching football skills (Moore & Williams, 1967) make any headway? It is suggested that the use of space, effort, body-shapes, rhythm, creativity, expression and movement can increase football ability. This is presented as an art-form. The view illustrates the possibilities of wide application of Laban's work but the idea does not present itself as operative unless it is handled with considerable expertise.

Programmed learning can individualize instruction in physical education. The inventive and imaginative use of programmed learning in achieving physical efficiency, coaching, work with slow learners and gifted pupils, and to increase motivation is possible. Curriculum content innovation must imply method change. The use of programmed learning has to be considered by the physical educationist and used where it serves his particular aims and objectives. It cannot be dismissed as inapplicable without thorough trial. It will not be suitable in every way; innovations rarely are in this category. The concept must be taken, tried and carefully evaluated. Here, controlled experimental conditions are particularly appropriate. The content of Laban's movement principles and his space-harmony concepts can all be presented in programme form - and be taught through this approach. Providing that this is accompanied by the relevant practical work and kinaesthetic experiences, there is nothing educationally unsound in this use of programmed techniques.

Margaret Streicher's (1970) work as a physical educationist in Germany is well-known and her work is now translated and available in English. She is in the Laban tradition though her approach appears to be more orderly and delineated than his. She has ideas for innovation grounded in generally accepted principles, and her perceptiveness in indicating the nature of development is remarkable. She refers to physical education as applied biology, and shows that the content of the curriculum in the future will be selected from a vast field of purposeful and art forms of movement. Those which are educationally valuable will be chosen and the experiences of the past will be essential as bases from which new curricula will develop. This states the Laban position exactly. His influence to date can never be negated. Whatever the course in the future, that which exists today will form its basis. The curriculum today is the launching-pad of innovation for the future.

Browne (1970) believes that Laban-trained physical education teachers have been too narrow in their work in schools. He sees them as eminently qualified to venture into Dance-Drama, and other inimitable, expressive media. Laban's work has given them a vocabulary of movement techniques which can be used to build functional or expressive sequences:

> . . . it follows, therefore, that any teacher trained in Laban's principles has the knowledge required for assisting children to create dance-like sequences.

This is the plea for integration once more; an argument for the physical education teacher to leave a narrow specialism and become associated with the wider field of the arts. When this happens, his influence on curricula planning will consequently be wider and the basic movement ideas will be incorporated into a greater proportion of the work encountered in schools.

Team-teaching is a developing educational trend, and one that physical education to date has not fully considered (Hendry 1972). New ideas in curriculum planning are using team-schemes. These will involve physical-educationists in accepting into their orbit, a wide variety of teachers from differing backgrounds. It is essential that this process takes place if physical education is to take its 'central' place. If other teachers are not brought into the physical education sphere, the subject will be left out on the periphery of curriculum organization. In any team-teaching venture, the physical educationist should have a significant part to play. The Laban-based observational techniques, knowledge of movement principles, and the use of intrinsically attractive material are all attributes that the representative 'team' should be pleased to include as part of their structure.

Many of the points raised concerning curriculum development are neatly summed up by Armytage (1972). He develops the view that curricula themselves should be collaborant, with all concerned helping to decide what they contain. Also, they need to contain an element of choice:

> The implications of choice are that the curriculum will have to

contain certain very carefully tailored options or courses which it has become fashionable to call 'modules' . . . Each option should be a survival pack of skills, techniques and practice that can be objectively assessed at the end of the time spent on it.

The ongoing nature of curriculum change is stressed, as is the need for negotiability in a revised system of higher education.

What is clear is that change is inbuilt in the educative process. In physical education, curriculum change is high in the order of priorities. As Laban's work has influenced change over the past three decades, so it will be a significant, if different, influence in the future.

Change
Change in physical education, through the use of Laban's ideas came about through these processes:

1   As a result of courses for teachers organized by the Ministry of Education, various university departments, and local education authorities.
2   Teachers who had attended courses developed their work through further sustained contact with the course organizers.
3   Trained students began to emerge from the Laban Studio.
4   The work was spread through the activities and magazine of the Laban Guild.
5   Similarly, local dance-circles publicized movement activities.
6   Good offices were available through Her Majesty's Inspectorate and local authority physical education organizers.
7   Financial help was available from individuals interested in movement education.
8   The women's specialist colleges of physical education took up the cause, and students were trained in Laban methods.
9   Laban's ideas were applied to gymnastics and 'educational gymnastics' came into vogue.
10 The climate in education was conducive to change and so the processes used were facilitated.

To the extent that planning occurs in the contents of the preceding list, then the introduction of Laban's work into schools was planned. There was, however, no 'grand design'. Following the traditional English pattern, there was no formal, overt central direction, but change was 'favourably received' by HMI. The time was right for change and the ideas in question were in line with the more individual, flexible approach characterizing change in education generally. The processes by which change took place are a perfect example of how development occurs in the English system. The roots are in the schools, directly in the hands of the teachers. These practitioners are encouraged by advisers; their work is admired; they are used for in-service training of others and so the process gathers momentum.

Dedicated individuals are important in this process. Elsie Palmer, a physical education organizer in Lancashire financed a meeting for chief education officers herself to try to interest them in movement education. Actually, on this occasion, only two turned up. Marion North published *A Simple Guide to Movement Teaching* privately, and distributed it herself. The book had developed from a postal course she had organized earlier.

First developments were very regional. The table (p. 96) confirms that the main centres were Lancashire and Yorkshire, and it was here that the first work in schools flourished. The London figure in the table is an 'establishment' figure rather than indicating schools activity of the magnitude of the Lancashire/Yorkshire work.

There had been great strides in physical education in the early thirties. The 1933 syllabus represented a significant forward move in its day but even at that time, 'A small group of teachers of physical education were questioning the very success in which they themselves were participating.' Folk and Greek dance, and Eurhythmics of many forms were in schools but for some, all these forms of dance excluded sufficient opportunity for children to express or communicate their own ideas in their own way (Jordan, 1966).

After thirty years since the first signs of a change in the approach to physical education began to appear, many rifts have appeared in the movement and many problems have been located. 'Confusion has arisen as the work has spread.' Much of this is centred in the movement/physical education controversy, a major issue which is examined later.

Incidence
Like all innovation in education, Movement has attracted

Analysis of the county of residence of
LAMG members from the membership list
published in the first issue of the Guild Magazine

County	No. of members	County	No. of members	County	No. of members
Abroad	5	Gloucester	4	Scotland	1
Beds.,	2	Hampshire	5	Shropshire	1
Bucks.,	1	Herts.,	1	Somerset	1
Berks.,	3	Kent	5	Staffs.,	8
Cambs.,	2	Lancs.,	30	Suffolk	1
Cheshire	3	Lincoln	2	Surrey	10
Denbighs.,	1	London	27	Sussex	11
Derby	4	Middlesex	5	Warwicks	20
Devon	2	Norfolk	1	Worcester	5
Dorset	1	Northants.,	1	Yorks.,	27
Durham	2	N. Ireland	1		
Essex	4	Northumberland	2		
Glamorgan	2	Notts.,	1		
		Oxford	2		

publicity. As a visual art which often contains an end-product which can be shown and which constitutes a 'performance', it has attracted the mass media. It is difficult to assess its incidence in schools. Some evidence can be offered by looking at research but this is inconclusive. Questionnaires are temptingly easy but they are notoriously unreliable and lack validity. Thornton's (1971) use of questionnaires is discussed in appendix two. With regard to research evidence, Owen studied a list of theses in connection with the study of physical education in 1965. Out of a total of one hundred and twenty, less than a dozen can be loosely described as being concerned with Movement, and only one of these has a stated, overt reference to the work of Laban. Owen produced a similar list in 1969. Here two hundred and seventy-six references were given. No more than twenty of these could be even remotely linked with Movement studies. Of these, seven were concerned with the work of Laban; a slight acknowledgement of rising interest. Howlett compiled a list of studies concerned with the art of movement which had been completed by 1969. Twenty-four titles are given here including American work. Of these, none have specifically examined the life, work and influence of Laban.

A study of the literature is probably as good an indication as it is possible to acquire. Personal experience and comment from informed sources is also productive, and although it is subjective, it may be none the worse for this.

The incidence of movement education in schools is much less than one would imagine. In fact a 'myth of movement' exists. There is evidence on this point from Bruce (1963, 1965) who writes:

> When one remembers that Mr Laban and Miss Ullmann came to England more than 20 years ago and considers the number of students from colleges who have experienced this kind of work in their training, together with the untiring efforts of a few people in advisory capacity in education, it would seem that in the senior school especially there has been slow progress in the development of the teaching of the arts of dance and dance/drama and that we should investigate possible reasons for this.

These reasons are suggested:

    1 insufficient knowledge of the students.
    2 lack of understanding from head teachers.
    3 the exploratory nature of the work.
    4 difficulties of evaluation
    5 the non-productive nature of movement.
    6 the failure to recognize children's changing interests.

A recent view on the subject is that 'Dance is still the Cinderella
of education and will remain so unless you, and especially you
who have so many opportunities, can show that it is the
primary and most basic element in education' (Jordan, 1972).
    The reasons for lack of development are that:

    Few people are confident and able to teach these arts without
    hesitation. Most are doubtful about the adequacy of their
    knowledge of movement and uncertain as to the relationship
    between dance, dance/drama, and the other arts.

If students feel inadequate in these areas after three years in
specialist colleges, there must be a query about parts of the
college curriculum. Is sufficient attention paid to the
identification of teaching strategies, interaction techniques,
personal teaching styles, and the job-content of the physical
education teacher?
    In a major review of physical education in England from
1900–1950 by Major (1969), there is no mention of Laban or
modern educational dance at all but there is one sentence
which is significant. The writer speaks of 'the interesting
experimental work which has been started in the primary
schools of various LEAs'. Had this lecture been given in 1950,
this would have been understandable. In 1969, the
interpretation must be different. Presumably the author saw
nothing important about this early innovation.
    Students applying for women's colleges offering specialist
physical education courses are a very select sample whose
school experiences in Physical Education could be expected to
be good. In one year, only four of the entrants at Anstey
College had any previous experience of modern educational
dance. 'The quality may indeed be good but the quantity is
disappointing' (Webster, 1969). At Lady Mabel College a
recent survey revealed that twelve students out of seventy-six

had experience of educational dance before entry to college. During interview, before coming to college the most popular answer to the question, 'Are you looking forward to your practical work?' is 'I'm a little worried about the dance as we don't do it at school.'

Ruth Foster, formerly Staff Inspector for Physical Education agreed with the 'myth of movement' suggestion. She thought the reasons for this were:

    i wastage from the profession
    ii the subject is undervalued by head-teachers
    iii a predominance of young teachers is involved
    iv if there is no Movement, no-one worries
    v frequent staff changes

She also thought that Movement asked children 'to expose' themselves and the teenage culture today does not do this readily. Miss Foster raised the fundamental issue of whether Movement is physical education. 'Physical Education sponsored Movement – it may well kill it.' The inference is for a separation of the two activities.

Webster (1969) refers to an article by Bantock and uses this quotation:

> There are two cultures, one for the intellectually élite and one for the average person . . . the latter must be taught more at the affective or feeling level – through art, music, dance and drama.

Webster does not even question this view but applauds it as 'university support' for the place of dance in education. Now whilst Bantock's view is tenable, it is personal and arguable. His strongly élitist position would be completely rejected by many educationists. Is Movement an activity predominantly for less-able children, the under-privileged, and the non-academics? If Bantock's view has wide adherence in schools, this could be a contributory factor to 'the case of missing movement in our schools'.

Every educational innovation attracts its bizarre elements. 'The role of modern dance in camping', and attempts to teach 'appreciation of posture' as a school subject are indeed peripheral. Does this kind of spin-off from a mainstream idea undervalue the core idea?

This book examines the incidence of movement in England

but the same factors are apparent in America (Weiner & Lidstone, 1969). Is this an unavoidable concomitant of the art? Are there intrinsic difficulties? The problem is examined in the next section.

Problems

The main difficulty inherent in studying the impact of Laban on Education in England is the problem which physical education and related disciplines have with semantics. It permeates every argument raised and has been widely recognized. Maslow (1968) commented that physical education was 'floundering in a semantic swamp'. When Shakespeare talked about, 'Words, words, words,' he implied a kind of discomfort and dislike of them. Terminology has bedevilled Movement Education studies. A preface for a book on Movement begins:

> This book is about an activity which has as yet so limited a vocabulary that it has not found even a distinctive name. It is, therefore, extremely difficult to write about. The difficulty arises in part because words and phrases familiar in one context are used in a different context with an extended meaning (Jordan, 1966).

The researcher is faced with a profession which cannot even define its core terms. Russell (1958) asked, 'What is implied in the term "movement"?' Over the years since that time a similar question has been asked and discussed in almost every book and at every conference concerned with physical education. The profession does not seem to be able to establish a base for progression. The same semantic wrangles persist and even today, one is always left, after discussion, with the feeling that 'we've been here before'. This, however, is no modern phenomenon. In 1924, Johnstone identified the problem when assessing the early efforts of Dalcroze teachers of movement and music in schools. She wrote:

> One becomes bewildered in trying to follow through the maze of words that which represents a thread of reasoning. The flow of language is intolerably copious and the phraseology is very involved.

Later, in 1938, Jordan was concerned about meaning and talked about, 'The too familiar tags – what do they all signify?' Evaluation in this professional setting is difficult.

Apparently, the profession is prepared to live with this problem. It has been described as 'a necessary evil – the problem of trying to describe a transient experience.' An important product of the words wrangle is the use of a particular terminology to describe movement. This has frequently taken the less serious student away from the fundamentals to superficial quibblings about jargon (North, 1971). In order to try to clarify these issues, physical educationists have sought the advice of the current educational philosophers. In the British Journal of Physical Education subject index for 1970, nine out of twenty-eight entries are philosophical/literary/theoretical. This is easily the largest classification and in an intensely practical subject, shows the size of this academic problem. Professors Peters, Bantock and Reid have been frequent contributors in the debate. Another result of the words controversy has been that many physical educationists have taken advanced diplomas in philosophy and have become embryo philosophers themselves. Far from clarifying the issue, the latter move has given experts in physical education more analytic tools which have raised additional problems more than solved those which already existed.

The main issues debated concern Movement in Laban terms. What do 'modern' and 'educational' mean in the term Modern Educational Dance? What actually constitutes physical education and what is its relationship to Human Movement Studies? What converted physical training into physical education? What are the aims and objectives of physical education? Do these differ from the main aims of Human Movement Studies? Should words which have common meanings be used in specific ways applied to movement studies?

Latest published material about modern educational dance (Redfern, 1973) is still primarily concerned with philosophical analysis of appropriate concepts and a discussion of the meaning of terminology. Objective and enlightened views of the use of Laban's work in Education are now given. Many similar points to those which have emerged in this study are being made elsewhere. The concern is that development should occur which springs from Laban's work and that the value of Movement in helping students to acquire the abilities noted in the upper levels of Bloom's hierarchical structure, namely the ability to discriminate, exercise choice, make judgements and evaluate should be explored. Rightly, problems associated with the many assumptions which have been made concerned with the idea that 'skill and creativeness in dance provides an appropriate base for creativeness and skill in other fields' need clarifying. This idea has little validity when it is assessed against what is known about 'transfer of training' and yet it has been at the base of many arguments concerning the place of Movement in Education. Although recent work establishes a new high in objectivity in modern educational dance, the use of philosophical analysis explodes the problems rather than contributes new thinking to solve them. Papers read at professional conferences still rake over the old ground rather than make radical re-assessments and suggest new blueprints for the future. The profession expects solutions rather than semantic debate – whether they will be forthcoming is problematical. This is a major problem and has meant that issues are usually blurred and solutions are rarely clear-cut.

Another difficulty intrinsic to the study is the problem encountered when the work of a man is evaluated shortly after his death. One is swamped by disciples with messianic allegiance. There is a tendency to close ranks to protect Laban's image, and to regard everything he said as gospel. This has occurred to many educationists, notably Dewey and Froebel. In the movement field, the same thing happened to the work of Delsarte after his death. His ideas were attenuated and his influence diminished. Similarly, Johnstone (1924) writes of the followers of Dalcroze:

> I think the exponents of the system have done it disservice by claiming for it too universally high results and by underestimating other methods and other teachers. They would have helped it more if they had been more restrained in their enthusiasm.

Huxley (1961) asserts:

> By those who serve him, a great man must be treated as a

mixture between a god, a naughty child, and a wild beast. The God must be worshipped, the child amused and bamboozled, and the wild beast placated, and when aroused, avoided.

This is good counsel for Laban's students who have not followed this advice. The values which Laban admired and which enabled him to formulate his principles – innovation, originality, flexibility, individual interpretation and use of the imagination – have been deprecated and left unrewarded, with the result that stereotypes have ensued. This has been recognized and the profession has been warned against 'any tendency to rigidity and too vigorous holding on to the outer form at the expense of inner content. Knowledgeable change, in Movement, is essential if our work is to survive. Every new year brings a new situation which cannot be handled as last year's problem' (North 1964a). In spite of this, old ways still persist and inhibit growth.

The work of Laban has influenced the education of girls far more than boys partly because of the historical accident that during the early days of the growth of Laban's influence, men were fresh from HM forces and still focused on military movements. Attempts have been made to rectify this but there is a persuasive school which does not accept Laban ideas uncritically as a vehicle for boys' work. In fact, Laban's devotees have spent more time in regularizing their position with girls and younger children than persuading others of the relevance of their work to older boys. A case has been made for a fair trial of new approaches and compromise, but warning notes have also been sounded:

> Likewise it seems unreasonable and undesirable that anyone trained and experienced in command-response techniques should adopt overnight a conversational method merely because the latter has been found to suit others (Randall, 1967).

It is not possible to generalize about Laban's influence on English Education in total. His influence on the physical education of older boys has been much less far-reaching than that on girls. Laban himself usually received a hostile reception at Leeds University when he talked to their diploma students. This point was substantiated by R. E. Morgan, formerly Director of Physical Education at Leeds University and agreed by Lisa Ullmann who said that the lack of acceptance by men of his ideas always worried Laban. There is undeniable bias on both sides of the 'boys/girls' argument. In a work of mighty proportions purporting to study the professional preparation of teachers of physical education, written in 1967, there is one paragraph devoted to the influence of Laban, and in the conclusions, no mention at all of a movement approach to physical education (Lewis, 1967). This work is written by a man and although the brief does not specify men's and boys' physical education, this is the way it has been interpreted. The bibliography in this study does not contain any books by Laban. The assumption is that the writer considered Laban wasn't important, or that up to 1967, he didn't play any part in the writer's brief. This unbalanced study illustrates a typical tripolarity – the devotees, the anti-Labanites, and those who pretend that Laban and a movement approach do not exist. The study in question belongs in the last category.

In conclusion, it is possible to deduce that the introduction of ideas into schools, based on Laban's theories, profoundly challenged the physical education world. It caused the profession to re-think its aims and objectives and sparked off a whole range of issues, trends and problems which are still being tested empirically today. The influence of Laban's work has not stopped with the introduction of work based on his thinking. He contributed to a fundamental re-think about the concept of physical education which is still fermenting today. The contemporary issues raised later are in no small way due to the influence of Laban over the preceeding three decades.

Justification

Proponents of Movement Education suggest that schemes based on Laban's principles act as a vehicle for both physical and intellectual development. What are the bases on which these assertions rest? Does work in school based on Laban's art of movement cater effectively for children's growth and developmental needs? What is the justification for including movement education in the curriculum? Is the evidence given in support of its inclusion purely intuitive and personal, or is there support for it from related disciplines as well?

'If mental processes can induce movement, why should not movement induce mental processes,' is often offered as the kernel of Laban's theories. Most justification for the inclusion of movement in the work of schools centres round this point. The Schools' Council Physical Education Committee gave as their objective in physical education that it should:

> . . . assist in the optimum, balanced growth of each individual by the development, not only of his physical resources and their skilled and efficient use, but also his capacity for creative and imaginative work.

Echoes of both these statements are seen throughout the literature.

> Movement experience is synonymous with growth . . . and is the starting point of all human activity. (Cheney & Strader, 1971)

> That action is not purely physical, mental or kinaesthetic but an agent for the stability required to profit from education. (Foster, 1960)

> Dance can be considered as the primary art because, firstly, it is an expression in movement which is itself the first expression of the human being; because secondly every other form of expression uses the universal language of movement as its vehicle. (Russell, 1969)

These assertions are the central ones advanced for movement education. They are arguments which place Movement as a link between cognitive and affective behaviour. It is an argument powerfully supported by Richard Hoggart (1971) in his Reith lectures. He showed the fundamentality of paralinguistics or non-verbal communication in helping people to adjust to the relationships needed in our society, where there is an important need to pick up the signals of posture, gesture, and facial set:

> We are like people who take part by ear in a very subtle non-stop symphony.

Implicit in Hoggart's view is the unity of action leading to ideas, and ideas leading to action - a basic Laban concept.

Physical educationists have been very concerned about the low status of their subject and its teachers. Consequently, justification of the subject has concerned them greatly. The split in the profession between 'the movement approach' and 'the physical education approach' has not helped them to make headway. There is insecurity in the profession because of this split and a need for conviction within the discipline before outsiders can be convinced. Movement ought to be the unifying factor which closes the ranks of the profession, say the Labanists. It is at the heart of all human activity and its use in education brings the whole personality into play in a balanced and integrated fashion. The originator (Russell, 1957) of this idea, however, asserts six years later in 1963 that 'one would have thought that there was no longer a need to sell the subject.' In 1969 she is once again deep in the justification debate.

Most of the views quoted have been attacked as loose and woolly, superficial and over-generalized. The move in recent times has been to justify the subject through an examination of aims and objectives, and through the development of taxonomies.

When objectives are seen in behavioural terms it should be possible to prepare a detailed, logically argued case for the inclusion of movement in the curriculum. Using curriculum development strategies, it is possible to demonstrate the need for movement education and show its role as an integrator in the educative process. Until now, little had been done along these lines and somewhat extravagant claims have been made for Movement (See Simpson, 1967). Recent work has redressed this balance and shown that movement education can enhance these values:

a   The development of individual and personal capacities.
b   Increasing social awareness.
c   Role-playing and practice in the group situation.
d   Increasing poise and confidence gained through self-mastery and awareness of one's body image (North, 1971).

However, caution is needed when trying to state results in terms of pupil behaviour:

A valid criticism can be made that too often in practice these values are simply not realised. Often the work is seen to be merely a bodily activity, divorced from any deeper meaning.

The physical education teacher portrayed by Barry Hines in *A Kestrel for a Knave,* illustrates the danger which North identifies. His aims were in terms of activity for its own sake without any clearly formulated reason for undertaking the exercise.

The goals stated above have not been reached. They are implicit in movement education based on Laban's work though, and they are attainable through a movement approach. The fact that they have not been reached cannot be attributed to the basic tenets. Here is an element of justification in theory, the practical attainment has yet to be fully realized. Again the question of controversy within the profession appears as North (1971) points out that:

> It is likely that our insecurity has delivered us over to the existing conditions which have the effect of limiting development in our own field.

Is Human Movement Study really two disciplines, one the academic study of human movement, the other, this study applied to the education process? Williams (1966) claims that the art of movement derives from dance and was adopted by physical education. Having attained maturity, it should become independent. He distinguishes 'education through movement for functional and recreative efficiency from education through movement as an art'. This view shows 'Movement' as a possible academic field of study, and separates 'dance-orientated' movement from 'educative-movement'. This is an important distinction taken up by several commentators. The issue is less important in the context of this book than the light it throws on Laban's influence on the thinking in the debate, and the importance which is attached to some form of movement education appearing on the curriculum. If physical education can be considered to be a practical theory, 'then we have a neat and acceptable way round a previously difficult situation and an answer to the discipline problem' (Webb 1972). The emergence of taxonomies in the Bloomian mould provides a solid base for justifying Movement in schools in that they can identify its theoretical content, look at evaluation procedures, and relate possible learning experiences to both the personal and social needs of pupils today.

In the educational atmosphere now, when concern for the individual in his social milieu is very important, the concern with both personal and social needs is a pertinent point of justification. More evidence on the points shows the relevance of movement to social needs in an increasingly sedentary society. Children's delight in movement, the corporate effort it generates and its importance as a means of non-verbal communication are stressed. All these points are important aspects of life-styles today and as such, ought to figure in curriculum planning.

The movement case can be supported by studying basic motivation. Laban's ideas on the central role of movement in life and as a basic human need, are compared with Ouspensky's belief that there are emotional and movement centres in the human being which control man's involuntary and impulsive actions, and that movement thinking is therefore in part, an orientation of those points of control which are outside the normal conscious and mental levels of thought. This use of what Freud called libido is highly speculative and very much a faculty theory but nevertheless, it illustrates an attempt at justification of the importance of movement which does draw on measurable scientific data more than affective intuition. Laban was interested in the work of Ouspensky so it is not surprising that their ideas can be linked in this way.

It is easier to link the developmental needs of younger children to movement than it is to establish a case for older children. Activity, incessant exploration, a questioning curiosity which involves a physical investigation of the environment, all have movement at their centre. James (1967), however, plays this down and shows that children have formed concepts of body awareness at about thirteen. What they need is to solve more abstract problems and use movement creatively to achieve their own degree of self-actualization; to use the movement vocabulary they have previously acquired to articulate their new interests and help to solve their adolescent problems more eloquently.

Langer (1953) establishes the movement case by stressing the need for full sensory experiences. As music caters for the auditory senses, so movement can express physical needs. Bantock (1971), a philosopher like Langer, stresses the re-ordering, as distinct from the relief aspect of therapy, and shows its relevance to intellectual development at both operational and pre-operational levels. Dunn (1970) and Ullmann (1970) link their justification to Herbert Read's (*Education through Art*) view that 'the senses are only educated by endless activity'. All primary learning comes from action. It is physical activity which sparks off intellectual activity and leads to growth and development. This is the natural endowment of children by which they achieve the different stages of maturation. Children need to acquire 'movement-sense' which is a general condition of motor sensitivity and competence. These views illustrate a dilemma. The statements are axiomatic and acceptable but they are offered without any supporting evidence. There is no research, no data, nothing concrete to help present the case and exception to the views can be taken on these counts. The movement writers and practitioners are vulnerable. Few of them present their arguments tightly enough to convince the 'psychometric lobby' in education which demands a more rigorous approach. One essential fact about Laban's work is that it has provided the basis for a scientific approach to the study of human movement. Few of his followers have used efficiently collected data, based on his principles, with which to support their case. Here is a significant lack and an area for research.

Professor Reid, another philosopher, is an ardent supporter of the case for movement education in schools. His argument is based on the premise that movement gives insights which are different in kind from the knowledge acquired in other scholastic subjects . . . in particular *direct* knowledge of meaning, unique unparalleled, untranslatable:

> Today, as the young revolt against the unreal and the artificial, something which is quite divorced from these two things like personal movement may fill a direct need . Reid (1970).

Movement, drama and the other arts can assist language development. Movement should be allied with Music and Manipulation as the 3 M's which are suggested (Foster, 1972a) as the new basic subjects in the curriculum. Foster shows that the skills subjects of the 3 R's grow out of the 3 M's in an integrated, inter-disciplinary approach to learning. A central place for movement in the curriculum is argued in the 'two-culture' theory, but in this élitist view, Movement is restricted to:

> Those children with whom our present system of schooling would appear to have failed (Bantock, 1971).

This theory is wholly relevant to the argument. It is not possible to quote fully but Bantock refers to:

> the movement education which Rudolph Laban has done so much to develop . . .

and places it as:

> the fundamental discipline of a revised educational system for those who found the culture of the book unacceptable. One can find no stronger argument for its inclusion in the curriculum than the statement which sees movement education as the catalyst force, the elixir which performs the transformation from anti to pro school.

But is it only for less able pupils?

Changing approaches draw heavily on support from child development, psychology, and philosophy. The centrality of movement in the curriculum is stressed and advocates have stopped trying to justify the inclusion of movement as a watertight subject, in its own compartment on the periphery of the curriculum. This is very much at variance with some earlier theories. It is odd that Laban himself in all his 1954 writings was arguing the case of movement as an integrating force when his followers are just acknowledging that this is its rightful place in the newer approaches to education especially the integrated, discovery methods of the primary and middle schools.

The work of the philosophers has been stressed. There is one more whose work is valuable because it combines clarity and lucidity with precision and directness – rare qualities in physical education literature. This is the work of Phenix in *Realms of Meaning* and it is a classic philosophical justification. It is quoted fully as it sums up what many others have tried to say. It is a synthesis of many views and a telling argument which pinpoints the role of movement in growth and development and its usefulness in catering for individual needs:

> The funadmental concept of the art of movement is the organic unity of the person. Health means wholeness, and the goal of education may be regarded as personal wholeness. From this standpoint, the classic duality of mind and body is rejected. A

person cannot think without a body, nor are his motor responses independent of thought. If learning is to be organic, provision needs to be made for activities in which the intellectual and motor components of experience are deliberately correlated. This union of thought, feeling, sense and act is the particular aim of the arts of movement and of the fields of health, recreation, and physical education. Nowhere else is the co-ordination of all components of the living person so directly fostered, nor the resultant activity so deeply rooted in the unitary existence of the person.

Laban's work is usually linked with movement and dance but he had a great influence on the teaching of gymnastics as well. Following the application of his principles to the teaching of gymnastics by Ruth Morison (1969) and her colleagues, 'Educational Gymnastics' became popular. Williams (1970) documents Laban's influence here saying:

> The Art of Movement made two great contributions to physical education. It showed how the teaching of gymnastics could be brought into line with modern methods and principles of education, and it gave the teacher an additional means of observation through the analysis of movement into the use of force, time and space.

The use of Laban's principles in gymnastics has released far-sighted physical educationists from the bonds of training to search for ways of fulfilling the educational ideals of meeting the needs of the individual. Educational gymnastics tries to realise the aim of recognizing movement as a fundamental condition of life. This is done by stressing body control and the attachment of tangible values. The value of the creative aspect of educational gymnastics and its link with self-set tasks which can be accomplished in an imaginative way to reduce needs is stressed. In the profession, Educational Gymnastics has severe critics. The issue is evaluated subsequently.

The education of disadvantaged young people ought to be based on their 'creative positives' (Torrance & Torrance, 1972). Compensatory programmes never really succeed while they are based on the pupils' deficiencies. Eighteen 'creative positives' that occur strongly and frequently amongst disadvantaged young people have been identified. Four of these are specifically concerned with movement, and eight more are clearly related to it. The latter are concerned with movement and the emotions, materials, role-playing, rhythm, speech, and skills in group learning. These are the former specific areas:

1 Enjoyment of and ability in creative movement, dramatics, dance, etc.
2 Fluency and flexibility in non-verbal media.
3 Responsiveness to the kinaesthetic.
4 Expressiveness of gestures, 'body-language', etc.

This study on 'creative positives' is based on observation in school and at play. It highlights children's natural activities and shows the part which movement plays in these. The aim is to increase problem-solving ability. The fact that movement studies are placed high in classroom provisions as a means of eliciting problem-solving strategies is powerful justification for its inclusion in the curriculum.

Psychological evidence

There is a body of knowledge from psychology which can be used in support of Laban's principles and their application to education. Laban (1954c) attempted to produce evidence but his lack of psychological training, coupled with his difficulties with the English Language make his efforts seem poor and open to severe criticism. In his work, when he tries to do this, he endeavours to make these points:

1 Movement provides a vehicle for the child's personal exploration, undirected and intrinsically motivated.
2 It stimulates intellectual activity.
3 It contains the open-ended qualities which permit individual application and development.
4 There are creative possibilities inherent in experimentation with movement – there is no one right answer but many acceptable positions.
5 There are aspects of movement which appeal to all – i.e. it may cater for the individual cognitive styles of everyone.
6 Lewin's theory that there is a basic need in humans to experience the resistance of objects and people implies movement.

7 Movement is an integrator of behaviour.
8 In view of the extraordinary strain of modern existence, there is a need for an adjustment which movement may help to provide.

Many of the points are made more specifically and scientifically by the developmental psychologists. It is from this school of psychology that most of the evidence in support of Laban accrues.

The work of Bruner is often invoked by writers such as Gilliom (1971), Murray (1968) and Russell (1965). In assessing the worthwhileness of Dance, Bruner's criteria:

> The test is whether, when fully developed, it is worth an adult knowing, and whether, having known it as a child makes a person a better adult,

is often used. The Labanist view is that dance takes its place in the curriculum because it satisfies this test. Bruner's ideas on the structure of knowledge relate to Laban's ideas on form:

> To learn structure, in short, is to learn how things are related.

Movement is taken to be central in this concept.

Movement is essential in the discovery approaches to problem-solving which Bruner advocates and one of his essential problem-solving strategies. Much the same point is made to link Maslow's 'self-actualization' with movement. The latter is an essential ingredient in the attainment of the former.

Piaget figures prominently in most psychological evidence. Much of the support suggested from him rests on his 'thought is internalized action' concept. This idea gives support to the link between movement and intellectual activity which Laban makes. An associated Piagetian concept is the view that motor action is the source from which mental operations emerge. There are obvious movement links here.

The beginnings of concepts, ideas and schemata are laid down through physical experience. Piaget's work shows that basic concepts such as space, time, shape, motion, speed, form and energy are all built up in this way and involve motor activity.

The attainment of ego-involvement in an activity is taken by Piaget to be beneficial. Self-chosen activities which ought to be a feature of movement education facilitate a high degree of ego-involvement.

The Piagetian concepts of assimilation, accommodation and adaptation are used in psychological justification of the links between movement and intellectual activity. The translation of experiences into conceptual understanding takes place through the mechanisms of assimilation and accommodation. These mental activities originate in action which involves movement. Therefore movement experimentations are often the birth of cognitive activity.

The fact that impoverished mobility adversely affects later intellectual functioning is eminently countable evidence as to the value of movement in releasing intellectual potential (See Dennis, 1960).

Several writers link the work of Hebb at McGill University with movement education. Hebb was concerned with the organization of behaviour and his work on the establishment of neural pathways is well-known. It can be linked to the Laban work by explaining it in terms of the Lichtenberg philosophy that 'What you have been able to discover yourself leaves a path in your mind.' Hebb's neural pathways may be better organized through a discovery approach involving physical interaction with the environment. Hebb and Piaget, in dialogue, found that they had much in common on this point. (See Tanner & Inhelder, 1953–56).

In a newly posed theory, creativity is seen as concerned with disturbing the status quo by acting on it individually to provide a certain sense of satisfaction appropriate to that individual. There are three levels of reaction suggested in the response with Movement occurring at all levels. Again, movement is seen as a basic ingredient, constant in a variety of creative responses at several psychological response-levels (Taylor, 1971).

According to Chesters (1950), movement helps to establish basic security and to achieve levels of satisfaction. The former comes through mastery of the body, and the latter through the pleasurable aspect of dance.

A study of the psychology of creative behaviour shows an emphasis on the hypothesized primary traits suggested by Guilford. These are fluency, flexibility, originality, elaboration, and inventiveness. All these can be engendered in good movement teaching. Similarly the 4 P's of creativity; process, product, person and press (environment) can also be catered for in a movement lesson.

Laban was interested in the work of the Gestalt psychologists. There are many points of contact between his work and theirs. Köhler's (1929) work in particular stresses the importance in behaviour of sensory organization, of which the kinaesthetic aspect is important. This is so important for Köhler that he believes perceptual judgements have a large dependence on it.

Vera Maletic is a leading dance figure in America, and has acknowledged her indebtedness to Laban. She was asked at interview (Halprin, 1967/8) . . . 'Of the main streams in psychology – Jungian, Gestalt, Existential, etc., which do you feel closest affinity with?' She answered, 'I feel most closely aligned with the Gestalt therapy, but that may be because of my contact with Fritz Perls. When I read his book, *Gestalt Therapy*, or when I work with him, I am continually reminded of similarities. It's the coming together of the parts. That is important to me, and it seems this is what is stressed in the Gestalt. I feel very identified with it.' Laban felt similarly. There is an affinity between movement students and the Gestalt view. The former are intrigued by the Gestalt and see movement of the human body as basic to the formation of the Gestalt, 'man in his body-space'.

In a psychological critique of Laban's *Die Welt des Tanzers*, Langer is concerned with what Laban called 'nucleation'. This emerges from tension, endures and then expires. It is a primary motivation and requires movement to make it physically perceivable. Laban conceived this idea purely in terms of mystic symbolism but in her philosophical analysis Suzanne Langer (1953) shows that it can be logically justified to her satisfaction, and that it is an idea which stands up under psychological scrutiny.

The generally accepted view now on transfer of training is that in essence, principles transfer while actual features of the process or function do not. There are many aspects of movement education for which transfer can be claimed, particularly those associated with aesthetic values. However, the degree of transfer which may take place is a thorny psychological issue; the most important variable in deciding the amount of transfer may be the teacher and her abilities (Garrison, 1964). Labanists have usually claimed too much for the principle of 'transfer'. More objective study can still reveal that principles of movement experience may transfer from one learning situation to another.

Trends

Movement education has currently reached a crisis point. The early, adventurous, imaginative approach flourished. It was conceived by dedicated enthusiasts and was fresh and spontaneous in schools. It developed and gained both ground and acceptance in the curriculum. Many of the opportunities for further growth were missed. The curriculum development movement, and its techniques and methods of examining curriculum decision-making only touched physical education, and particularly movement, in a peripheral manner. Now, there is a need for a fundamental re-think of the nature and purpose of movement education. The situation is right for the next creative breakthrough to achieve more apt educational aims and cater more effectively for the changing needs of children in a society whose values are altering so quickly.

Laban was perceptive enough to see the problems ahead in 1947. He wrote in the first edition of the Guild magazine, 'A living man is apt to err and to *develop*.' He stressed that his own thinking was extremely on-going and likely to change. He cautioned against set systems and methods. Had he been alive today, his approach may have been vastly different.

Several years ago Clegg (1965) saw physical education at the crossroads. He believed that it had to develop, integrate with other subjects, and be used as means of enriching experience or 'rightly lose caste and certainly lose educational effectiveness.'

The crisis is also noted in showing that the history of the subject has been a struggle for recognition. 'The teachers of physical education have had to pull their specialism up from its origins as a cheap cure for malnutrition into an integral and important part of the education of a complete human being.' This struggle is still on and has not yet been won (Britton 1972).

What has happened is that much movement education has become stereotyped; often it is a charade, carefully played out by the teacher and the class, where everyone knows their role and its expectations. It has followed a philosophy of the same thing for everyone, summed up by the 'ticky-tacky' of the folk lyric, 'And they're all made out of ticky-tacky and they all look just the same.' The necessity is for Movement to extend the pupils' thinking beyond its kinaesthetic context so that they see its relevance to life, and use it as an aid to general problem solving. Laban's role was as an innovator, an ideas producer and a 'first-stage-rocket-man'. He provided no answers. The answers must be found personally, by individuals, both teachers and pupils alike making their own relevancies and connections. The principles of movement must extend beyond techniques or systems which so often become 'closed' in psychological terms. Creative use of Laban's principles will create 'open' systems, whose chief characteristic is their ability to change and remain flexible in the hands of all who use them.

Early critics of Laban are becoming more objective. From total rejection, the counsel is now that dance experiences should be more 'outward-looking' as well as 'inward-feeling' (Munrow, 1972). This view can be equated to those already given. There is a need to consider dance in education as a means of giving something more than personal therapy, emotional satisfaction and an aesthetic experience. The stress can quite easily be channelled to more catholic aims, catering differently for each individual. If the chance of movement experience is provided, it may be accepted by both sexes, in the future, as part of a way of catering for individual needs and as a part of what it has become fashionable to call, 'doing one's own thing'.

In a provocative book which is aimed at helping students to become teachers using techniques more generally associated with the ad-man, Charles (1972) hammers home a relevant point with the aid of a catchword and mnemonic called GAR. This is an attempt to highlight the influence of 'body-talk' in the learning and teaching processes. Charles believes that body-talk is an under-used variable in helping the teacher and the learner. He advocates that more attention be paid to posture, gesture and facial set. This is a relatively new book, published in 1972. On examination, it has much in common with those ideas propounded by Laban and his pupil Warren

Lamb on this subject over twenty years ago. GAR stands for Guides, Accepts, Rejects. These are behaviour categories which Charles uses to help the teacher and the learner to perform their respective tasks better. The approach borders on the gimmicky but the use made of movement to aid understanding on the part of the learner, and efficient working on the part of the teacher, shows an imaginative development of a branch of movement education as yet little developed in England. The syndrome of movement studies abounds with growth points which await imaginative use. One way these may be identified and developed is through a use of brainstorming techniques in seminar groups formed from physical educationists with good traditional training but who are intent on the further expansion of their sphere.

There is a need for curriculum decisions to be based on clarification of aims and objectives, structuring of content and learning experiences, and realistic appraisal of teaching methods and contexts of learning. It is significant that in a review of trends in the curriculum of the primary school, a recent article (Richards 1972) does not even mention physical education. The author was questioned about this omission. He described Dienes work on the process of curriculum renewal. Dienes suggests a play/experimental stage, followed by a directed and purposeful stage where there is no clear realization of what is being sought, and lastly a practice stage necessary for fixing concepts where goals are clearly identified. He suggests this model provides a good analogy, and that the spread of Laban's ideas has now reached the second stage. 'Teachers are beginning to feel that they have been a little too aimless for too long.' He stressed teachers' needs for progression and to feel that their teaching was leading somewhere. The Schools' Council Humanities Project and recent work on objectives in education both provide similar models to those outlined earlier. Physical Educationists must be more concerned with this approach. *The Journal of Curriculum Studies* has been a barren ground for the researcher looking for physical education studies. Similarly, *Education for Teaching,* a recognized platform for curriculum innovation in colleges of education contained no articles specifically concerned with the physical education curriculum for a decade.

Future developments in movement education will include an increase in the use of movement in therapy. Through the years, some experimentations have taken place and a therapeutic role has often been suggested for the dance teacher. The need for research into movement therapy has been advocated by many writers who have shown that psychotherapeutics can emanate from a movement base when skilled staff are used. Movement classes with schizophrenics have been reported upon and the use of dance-drama as a form of occupational therapy with psychiatric patients has been described. Geneticists have been interested in Laban's work and show the possibilities for development when educationists and medical staff work together. All this work has been unco-ordinated. Little has been done on a national level but the growth points are there. In special schools, therapy through movement is a developing field whose growth depends on more trained workers. This could be an area for course development in specialist physical education colleges in a post-James organization.

Valerie Preston-Dunlop opened the Beechmont Movement Study Centre as a private venture. It failed for a variety of reasons, finance being the most important. However, the work done there in kinetography suggests this area as a growth point for future development. As this may occur in higher education, the point is taken up again later.

Laban's work has greatly influenced the Keep-Fit movement (Meier, 1966). Miss Eugenie Fraser, Chairman of the Training Panel of the Keep-Fit Association showed this clearly at interview as she demonstrated the use made of Laban's principles in helping to train Keep-Fit leaders. Many of these classes have now moved into the further education orbit, and the work has been linked to the Duke of Edinburgh's award scheme. In the expected age of recreation and leisure, this activity will probably figure more prominently in state-education at the tertiary level. Similarly, in an age of increased time for pleasure, there could be some updated revival of choral dancing as Laban introduced it into Germany in the 1920's.

Physical education is still essentially practical in schools. Classroom periods of physical education each week have been suggested many times. The profession is divided on this point and only a clarification of terms, aims and objectives will elucidate whether this is an appropriate forward move.

The teacher of physical education in secondary schools has traditionally been trained in a specialist college. There is now increasing use of other teachers who have expertise in activities, and the range of these options makes it impossible for one teacher to cover everything. In the future, physical educationists will come from atypical backgrounds and this may provide an infusion of new ideas and talent and lead to a widening of the more traditional view of the subject. (See Foster, 1972b). The links between physical and intellectual activity have already been discussed, as has the place of physical education in the curriculum. A recent movement in America throws some light on the approaches which may be adopted in bringing physical education into the core of curriculum construction. At the University of Syracuse, a department of Synaesthetic Education has been inaugurated:

> Synaesthetic education involves multisensory perception, not by means of vicarious experiences but through the learner's direct experience of his own reactions, ideas and feelings.

The basis of this approach is that all sensory experience contributes vitally to learning. What is called a 'heterogeneous conglomerate' of experience is integrated in a symbolic way into a harmonious whole. Synaesthetics aims to experience this whole. In movement education this becomes a plea to value a range of kinaesthetic processes which assist learning, and to arrange for these to happen as part of the learning experiences provided for children. Synaesthetics recognizes the value of movement education as an essential activity in learning. From the work at Syracuse, new evidence to support the case of a movement approach may emerge.

The points made lead to a conclusion that there is a need for more research into the aims and objectives of movement education, possible methods of evaluation, selection of learning experiences, and the use of approaches geared to individual needs. These points have been identified along with others. In observational studies the difficulties of objectivity in evaluation have been highlighted. The evanescent nature of movement being the main reason given. In 1963, it was indicated that movement research should be linked with inquiries in the field of child development and learning processes in order to gain effective substantiation of modern educational dance in the curriculum (Russell, 1963/4). There is little evidence after ten years that this suggestion has been taken up at all. The pattern in America is the same. Hawkins (1967) writes:

> We should have research that gives greater insight into the effective ways of developing movement potential. For example: How would the application of the principle of reciprocal innervation affect the development of flexibility in contrast to the traditional method of increasing flexibility through bouncing.

Whilst agreeing with the principle expressed by Hawkins, the specificity of the example suggests a further alienation of the researcher and the practitioner. The research required must have direct relevance to the curriculum problems faced by teachers. Recent pleas have been made for a good public relations arrangement between the profession and the public. A guard is necessary against the same thing being required within the profession.

The research required may not be the province of the academic researcher. One of the future developments must be that the practising teacher is involved in her own research programmes. Breakthroughs are just as likely to come from the carefully recorded perceptive observation of the teacher in the school, as from formal research, carried on in sterile objectivity, based on untested, poorly-validated academic hypotheses. The detailed observation by teachers of pupils' activities has provided growth before, and may still do so again.

Future development demands action. The literature abounds with exhortations for innovation, research and development over the last decade. Even in 1971, we read:

> . . . obviously further systematic research is needed to investigate areas of human response and human behaviour in movement terms (Corlett & Webb, 1971).

The need is for experimentation and reports stemming from this. Empirical study is required. The colleges of physical education can support research projects to carry out and evaluate imaginative curriculum development. Apart from isolated occasional papers coming from two colleges, little is done. The growth of BEd degrees in Movement Studies gives a splendid opening for this to happen. At present there is a move to require extended studies involving empirical inquiry in many universities. As this spreads, the results ought to feed back into the mainstream of innovation in schools.

SECTION B
Opposition and Support

Introduction

An effective case is made against the use of Laban's work in schools, and in assessing his influence on English Education, it is important to examine this contrary view. Is this case against Laban valid? What are the flaws in his work and the use which has been made of it? Where has impact been made which is particularly suspect and open to professional questioning? What movements are afoot to change areas of influence which are in question? As opinion is polarized and two camps emerge, is there a possibility of rapprochement between the two parties? Does a dichotomy in fact exist, or is it basically a lack of communication and semantic definition which makes it appear to be apparent? These are the questions which arise from examining the validity of 'the case against Laban' and the counter-argument.

Some of the criticisms of work based on Laban's principles stem from the extravagant claims which have been made for it, and the innocent way that some of Laban's disciples have presented their ideas. A great deal of the copy in the Laban Art of Movement Guild Magazine invites adverse comment. It is over-generalized, contains sweeping statements, is often sickly and cloying in its terminology, and smacks of veneration of the master and his works. Statements like:

> Rudolph Laban believes and *has proved* in his work with his vast numbers of pupils, patients and followers, that through the study and the practice of harmony of movement, the sense of values is stimulated and heightened. (Ullmann, 1964).

In the field of human behaviour, investigators rarely 'prove' anything; and certainly equally rarely ever claim to have done so. This naïve assertion is unacceptable to educationists today and gives grist to the arguments of dissidents. Similarly, one reads that:

> *Every* school and *every* college of education is working on Laban's principles in the gymnastics and dance work (Moore, 1971).

This is patently untrue and a piece of irresponsible nonsense to present in print. The same article contains other factual inaccuracies which invite adverse comment. Diana Jordan did not work with Laban in Germany, and Ruth Foster was not 'chief of staff HMI'.

Many of Laban's most ardent supporters have seen his work as the panacea of all educational ills. The same is true of 'Creativity'. Both contributions are rendered a disservice when these outlandish claims are made for them. Arnold (1968) makes this same point and concludes:

> However, despite the sometimes fanciful claims made on its behalf, it is an important factor in education in general, and physical education in particular, if talk of balance, individuality and personality integration is to have any meaning at all.

In 1970, an article in the *British Journal of Physical Education* by Corlett (1970) created comment. It was bogged down with the minutae of movement, and was grossly wordy and unclear. One passage began:

> Movement tasks stress the qualitative aspect of motion bringing an awareness of how the action is occurring through demanding a mental concentration to sense and control the natural flow of movement.

The author elucidates this point – an eminently sensible and necessary course of action, but she becomes more open to criticism than ever as she asks:

> Did John/Jane fulfil the movement task on the floor? What was his/her answer to the problem? Has he/she learnt to control his/her body-weight coming down to the floor? Where and how did he/she work during the climax of the lesson on apparatus?

This contribution can only merit the label 'twee' and does the Laban case no credit. It provokes this kind of reply.

The obsession with Time, Weight, Space, and Flow, and paying homage to Mr Laban begins in the colleges of (physical) education . . . Many female students leave college fairly conversant with the mysticisms involved in the quality and quantity of movement, and they have undergone a thorough training in order to observe John/Jane's left leg pushing against the floor, and where John/Jane's hand goes while John/Jane is in the air. However, when the recently qualified physical education teacher attempts to organise the physical education programme and time-table, or organise an inter-schools' athletic meeting, she may find such training of little value (Ferdinand, 1970).

This was supported subsequently by this definitive last word on the subject:

At last a patch in the Labanistic clouds,

writes Myrle James (1971). She attacks the humourless approach, the language style, and the trite, superficial nature of the questioning as illustrated. She paraphrases the style to press home the case. 'Could/might some/all children/ colleagues think/imagine I/we am/are out of my/our tiny Chinese mind(s)?' The point is made. From such as this, there develops criticism.

Philosophical criticism
The writings of Laban have been criticized for their vagueness, mysticism, obtuseness and fantasy qualities. In the same article, he can range freely and ingenuously over anatomy, physiology, body types (somatotyping), the nature/nurture controversy, locomotion, colour, shape, rhythm, achievement, competition, the psychology of play, recreation, creativeness, and natural science (Laban, 1958). From this background, he educes an argument for movement as 'the great integrator', the nexus of education. It is against this background that philosophers have criticized his work.

Most of the philosopher's objections to Laban's work concern the unintelligibility of his writing, and the general air of pondering abstraction which it contains. Curl (1967a) believes that all Laban's writing suffers from these defects and says:

All of Laban's writings in English share with his German texts a large measure of obscurity. From 'Modern Educational Dance' 1947, with its undefined and often ambiguous teaching terminology, to 'Choreutics' 1966, with its highly abstract geometrical symbolism, we are faced with the same problem – mystical allusion: and when we review Laban's published lectures and articles, we reach the very peak of what Professor Langer has called 'a mystic metaphysics that is at best fanciful and at worst rapturously sentimental'.

There is little evidence in Laban's writings to support the view that he was 'a philosopher, a man of intellect, a scientist or a researcher' in the accepted sense of these words. Earlier, some of Curl's censures have been criticized but here, his case is absolute. A careful study of Laban's work does reveal all the inadequacies which Curl notes. There is a philanthropic quality about his writings, and a measure of scriptural authority which is hard for questioning students to accept. He draws without acknowledgement from the sources referred to in part two until his pronouncements appear to his followers to have the character of divine utterance.

In physical education today, there is a call for more empiricism. In fact, much of Laban's work is rooted in empiricism. The criticisms levelled at his approach can be summarized:

> The empiricism of Laban was romantic rather than scientific. It depended on inadequately defined and half-understood pseudo-religious concepts, instead of being built on quantifiable data.

This is the sad fact. Sad because the principles enunciated by Laban do provide the starting point for rigorous scientific enquiry. In his writings, Laban the artist, the romantic, the mystic always took over. These facets ousted Laban the brilliant observer, the taxonomist, the time and motion consultant. Instead of stating his data plainly, he imbued it constantly with mystic symbolism. On reflection this appears to be the fundamental weakness of his work which has led to severe criticism from philosophers.

It is important to report on one more part of Curl's inquiry. In a 1968 article, he concerns himself with Laban's writings on crystallography. This was a topic which fascinated Laban from boyhood and he refers to, 'the glorification of the great and general order of crystalization'. Curl calls this work 'bizarre', and is critical of Laban's attempts to link man's movements and dance gestures with crystals and motions of the universe. He regards the work as specious and as having no basis in human science. Laban's approach to crystallography is that of the fanciful amateur. His findings are at best highly speculative, and at worst 'crystal-gazing'. Lange (1970) examined Curl's criticisms and Laban's views on the nature of the crystal in detail. He believes that Laban 'quite certainly did not intend to create a new system of anatomical analysis of the human body.' Lange's view is that Laban's use of crystals is to be seen solely in relation to functional aspects of human movement. This is a relevant point for this brief. Curl does not attack this aspect of Laban's work on crystals. It is significant that this is the use which is made of crystal structures in education. Laban's application of crystal shapes to body movement is used in depth study of the art of movement in schools. It provides a working framework for the explanation of principles, and the scales of human movement. It provides the student with reference points which aid understanding and simplify difficult concepts. The use of crystallography in these terms is not in dispute, and it is the main use of the subject in education. The mystical use of crystals and their cosmic significance can be relegated to interesting biographical material. It is the use as outlined which is acceptable and valid in education.

All Laban's writings before 1939 must be recognized as the work of an artist and not an educationist. Also, his work in Germany must be seen in its socio-economic, and cultural context. At that time, in artistic circles, symbolism and mystic stresses were common. The difficulty of interpreting Laban's writings often comes from the metaphoric German in which he wrote. This was also fashionable at that time. If he were writing today, his style would be different.

Laban's early writings can be classified into two categories (Lange, 1969):

1 Personal attitudes as an artist of the expressionistic period of European art.
2 Objective exposition of the principles of movement.

The philosophers criticize the first category but in fact, it is the second which has real educational implications and value. What matters is his theory of movement and its application to education.

It is a common thing for a man's work to be evaluated, after his death, by detailed analysis of his ideas. This is often done in a destructive manner when the constructive thing to do would be 'to look more deeply into the wholeness itself'. Sir Fred Hoyle has described this type of negative analysis as akin to dissecting the goose that is laying eggs of gold in order to see what is causing it to happen. Constant reference by pro-Labanists to the concept of unity, and implying synthesis, integration and wholeness – notoriously vague ideas – does nothing to elucidate the problem or satisfy the critics.

Much of the philosophical objection to Laban's work is not relevant to this study. Significantly, the only aspect which is really concerned with this brief, namely the application of Laban's theories to education, is not dealt with at depth by the philosophers. It is clear that what they are attacking are some vague generalizations and unsupported mystical hypotheses. These, however, are not necessary adjuncts to Laban's analysis of movement applied to schools. There is little evidence of any inadequacy in Laban's theory of movement from the philosophers, and their attacks on his more fanciful ideas should not detract from his real achievements. If the mystical metaphysics lead to 'uncontrolled self-indulgence' in the educational applications, then there is a danger. This, however, is not really proven. It is a point to be guarded against and one which may require care in the future.

The work of Susanne Langer (1953) has been referred to obliquely. In both *Feeling and Form* and *Philosophy in a New Key*, Langer mentions the work of Laban and comments on his theories. She regards much of his work as capricious and ostentatious. When she has demonstrated this, however, her criticism is by no means total. She dismisses some of Laban's work as:

at best fanciful, and at worst rapturously sentimental.

Then, she shows Laban's work in a new light if one conceives dance:

. . . as a field of virtual powers - there are no actualities left in it at all, no untransformed materials, but only elements, living beings, centres of force, and their interplay.

In this view, Dance is a complete and autonomous art, the creation and organization of a realm of virtual powers. It has an intrinsic value of its own, implicit in its creation which may be its own justification. It is 'an expression of the soul'. Several movement theorists (Brown, Simpson and Allenbaugh) besides Laban have identified this quality in Dance which Gilliom (1971) calls its foundational aspect. It is a difficult concept however, and one which Gilliom suggests is only vaguely understood by most classroom teachers and movement specialists. Is it necessary for those practitioners to understand this philosophical basis in its abstract entirety? A full knowledge of it will not make them better teachers. What they require is a firm understanding of the basic movement concepts to enable them to plan creative stimuli, and observe intelligently so that they can use this observation to further continuing imaginative response and development on the part of their pupils.

Methodological and practical objections

The nature of education means that it is always open to reform and the zeal of particular sectional interests wishing to further their own causes. At present, curriculum development is vogue generally and specifically in physical education but sectional interests have now sometimes reached epidemic proportions. The arguments have resolved themselves on one side into the establishment of a case against Laban Movement. Those concerned with the acquisition of skills have attempted to show the value of this to the exclusion of a movement approach and seen the latter as something of a threat. Spearheaded by Munrow and Randall, they believe it is unfortunate to regard Laban's movement principles as a complete answer to the problem of skills acquisition. It must be only a lunatic fringe who do this, however, and this view is not at the heart of a movement approach. It is not a view to be found anywhere in the writings of either Laban or his principal interpreters. In fact, the ideas of Laban can be fused with those of his detractors. The argument against Laban is resolved into a compromise when the specific part which Laban's work can play in skills acquisition is acknowledged:

> In fact, no discussion of modern ideas in physical education is complete without reference to both Laban's principles and to Munrow's classification and detailed analysis of skills.

Munrow has been critical of much of the work based on Laban's thinking in the past but his recent work published in 1972 shows a more balanced view of the controversy. Now, he acknowledges the part played by Laban in the total pattern of physical education development in a more specific manner. He applies many of the strictures noted in this study, and picks out for comment many of the writings used here. However, he does not now dismiss, or refuse to recognize that a movement approach to skills acquisition can have a place in certain circumstances. Over the years, the change in Munrow's views is considerable. In some ways, it is microcosm of the change in attitude of many commentators who have been in broad opposition to the Laban school over the years. Now, the controversy rests more on specific, rather technical points more than on an argument intent on destroying approaches with a movement basis.

Controversy is not only confined to a dichotomy between skills and dance. Differences exist within these fields. Russell (1963/4) draws attention to an article in the *Times Educational Supplement*, *Dancing in the Dark*, and the correspondence resulting from it. She deplores the fact that fully trained dance (ballet) teachers are not recognized as qualified under the Burnham regulations whilst those students trained at the Laban Art of Movement Studios have recognition. She shows that 'there are many types of dance and many forms of modern dance – the Laban principles being a valuable but small part of an overall pattern'. The question of recognition for salary purposes is important and this article highlights an interesting topic. It must be difficult for trained ballet teachers to accept the distinction as made. What is special about the Laban training which brings recognition? The answer lies in the centrality of movement in education as seen by the Department of Education and Science and their advisors. Recognition in this context is the seal of approval, the official accolade. It is the ultimate justification set against a financial criterion, and formally acknowledges the influence of Rudolph Laban on English Education. In a capitalist, materialistic, acquisitive society, financial reward is one of the ultimate signs of acceptance and a telling argument against some of the cases advanced against Laban.

Writers, lecturers and commentators have criticized the methodology of movement teaching. This criticism is obviously concerned with the use which teachers have made of Laban's principles and the way they have applied them in schools. The attitude to Modern Educational Dance is changing and the subject is now generally accepted for its educational value but despite the large numbers of students attending dance courses in colleges 'the problem today is that there is still very little taught in schools' (Russell, 1961). This view has been examined in an earlier section when the incidence of movement teaching was discussed. Although the article was written a decade ago, the argument is still valid, and it brings the question of methodology to the fore as one of the possible causes of the failure to develop movement education. The personal nature of movement, its immediacy and transient quality present grave problems for the beginner. It is not easy to become a catalyst in the creative process involved in a movement experience.

Another methodological problem concerns the use of props, audio and visual aids, and other effects as stimuli. Can these be handled optimally by inexperienced teachers? In fact, should they be used? Should they be used partially, to support other approaches? The most important question concerns individuality and creative response. Does their use with a group effectively ensure failure for some? If we recognize individual cognitive style, if we understand associational cues to creative response, can a single form of stimulus succeed with a group? If a range of stimuli are required to spark off pupils who are predominantly audile, tactile or visile for example, can a teacher provide these? Is the plea not for an individualization of stimulus which is beyond the average teacher at present? These views bring into focus the whole concept of group response, and group involvement. How does a teacher cater effectively for a group who will make a joint response if she cannot cater optimally for each individual in the group? Are individual needs perforce sacrificed in group response situations? What should be the incidence of group to individual response in view of the points raised? What is their comparative importance in catering for individual and group needs? These many questions are concerned with method and with the philosophy of movement education. To deal specifically with method, they are unresolved today. Not only are they unresolved, they are unresearched and frequently undiscussed and unidentified. They may even be un-acknowledged by some teachers. The colleges have turned out practitioners often with a complete methodology – a survival kit which becomes trapped in its own limitations – one is tempted to say in its own kinesphere! There is a need for students to be trained with a far greater understanding of the nature of creative behaviour, and the role which open-systems play in this. Until they are 'at ease with unsolved problems', flexible, accepting, willing to accept change as a fundamental condition of their art, they will be faced with a series of question marks concerned with the validity of their approaches. Teachers who emerge from college as identikit products of a Laban system will have real difficulty in coping with conditions in schools today. Successful movement work is drawing more and more on a variety of bases, styles and approaches. Laban, per se, produces the straitjacket; Laban et al produces a more creative and imaginative response which may have more pupil-appeal.

A case has been made for the integration of the education and physical education components of the college course, to try to achieve a firmer liaison between the philosophical, psychological and sociological bases of education and the practical and theoretical study of physical education (Foster, 1972c). Methods used can never be fully effective unless the teacher is an educationist first and a physical educationist subsequently:

> It may be possible to study movement . . . without studying that which moves. It is not possible either to study or to teach physical education without first studying the child to be physically educated. A student of movement (art or science of) may or may not be a teacher of physical education; a teacher of physical education cannot help but be a student of children moving.

Flexibility, fluency and originality of movement in movement sessions in school are rightly applauded. These attributes are encouraged by teachers through a battery of teaching skills and strategies, one of the foremost of which is an exhortation:

> to find another way of doing a particular activity. This is laudable as a process but too often accepted as an end. In using this technique, too few teachers know how to reject the often trivial answers to the problems set (Webster, 1969).

How is progression ensured? How does the teacher teach skills without inhibiting creative response? How does she direct without telling, achieve the conformity required to ensure basic order and organization and still preserve an atmosphere which encourages creative response? How does she become:

> removed and yet present, concerned and yet not an inhibitor, the provider of some ideas, and yet the elicitor of more? (Foster, 1971a).

The analysis of these teaching skills as applied to movement education has not really been attempted in formal terms. The interaction analysis procedures developed from the work of Amidon and Hough (1967), Flanders and their associates offers one way of doing this. The original emphasis on verbal interaction needs to be supplemented to spotlight non-verbal responses but the use of the core technique presents possibilities for development. There are other techniques; the use of micro-teaching for example. There is an indisputable need for analysis if methodology is to progress and movement education is to expand and take its place at the centre of the educative process. This suggestion is greatly removed from a recent textbook approach for students which begins:

> The core of the book is a suggested syllabus given year by year, and based on the sixteen basic movement themes as set out by Laban in *Modern Educational Dance* (Russell, 1969).

Laban would not have approved this direct application of his sixteen principles to a set syllabus in the educational climate of today.

Some particular objections have been raised to the use of Laban's work in schools. In the mid-1950s, when movement was beginning to establish itself in schools, much was claimed for 'Movement' but all the literature concerned only 'Dance' (Randall, 1967). Modern educational dance is the aspect of movement stressed in most schools today but movement is generally *justified* in basic terms and *applied* in dance concepts. This is another reason for the failure of movement education to make headway. The 'dance' element has been an alienating factor, particularly for many men in the profession.

Laban ideas of 'transference of weight' and 'effort qualities' are more suitable for generalized skill training than anything else, and yet, their main use is not in this field. Laban saw basic movement as the foundation for all physical skills. However, as before, he offers no experimental evidence to support this view. There is considerable psychological evidence to the contrary if one examines concepts of transfer of training and the psychology of the acquisition of perceptual-motor skill.

Munrow (1955) questions the appropriateness of applying movement principles *outside* the context of modern educational dance. Many of the criticisms against Laban are similar but here Munrow differs from others. These intra-discipline differences, splitting even advocates of similar principles have been a feature of the debates in physical education through the years. Even seventeen years after these issues were first raised, they are comparatively unresolved. The worry is that the debates are carried on in an emotionally charged atmosphere, where intuitive judgements are made on little direct evidence, and where sectional interests are closely guarded.

In a later paper, Munrow (1955, quoted in 1972) severely questions the application of Laban's ideas to boys' physical education but does acknowledge its importance for both sexes at the primary level:

> I am all for trying to enlarge the Movement vocabulary of youngsters and I would have thought that free-dance, music and drama were the vehicles through which it was best achieved.

He doubts its wholesale acceptance later:

> Our children who learn through trial and error, and through exposure to situations learn in a wholly admirable way. But it is a slow way, and not suitable to the acquisition of refined techniques.

These criticisms are still aired today. The question asked is:

> Is discovery learning an economical way to learn skills where particular techniques need to be acquired which are identifiable and able to be broken down into their component parts for instruction?

Research which examines this problem is widespread but there is little in the discipline of physical education. This is another barren field where minimal objective evidence exists to elucidate one position against another.

The activity influenced by Laban which has been criticized most is undoubtedly educational gymnastics. The arguments centre around the points raised by Munrow:

> Are they (the pupils) going to find this the quickest and most appropriate approach to skill learning or are they going to be lost in harassed contemplation of their own Movement rather than sensing the enjoyment of early achievement? (Roberts, 1953).

Another early criticism levelled against educational gymnastics is that it raises difficult questions of levels of response. 'Also the children of today are rightly not expected to go on 'till they bust, but the tendency is often to give up before they have had enough. This is one of the problems of informal teaching in the hands of mediocre teachers' (Randall, 1956). The general gymnastics effects of mobility, strength and endurance are not enhanced by an educational gymnastics approach based solely on movement principles. If this is so, it raises the whole question of standards in the subject. Labanists have few acceptable answers to the question of standards of performance in educational gymnastics. Their aims centre on enjoyment and participation. They are vulnerable to severe criticism when they do not extend pupils with the ability to reach high levels of attainment. They are vulnerable when they present work for demonstration which has been developed for personal pleasure and intrinsic satisfaction. They are vulnerable when they attempt uniformity of movement in a group and fail to use any of the recognized techniques for achieving this.

'Standards of achievement' concerns many who criticize educational gymnastics:

> Although generally speaking, gymnastics work in the primary school has been based on Movement lines for a number of years, the standard of achievement has remained depressingly low (Severs, 1969).

The comments which have to be made on this issue concern evaluation and measuring techniques. By what criteria are results evaluated, and are accurate measuring instruments available to do this? In some quarters, the question is asked:

> Why measure at all?

The implication of the latter question is that there are no reasons for trying to quantify aesthetic, creative experiences. The opposing view is that whenever one teaches, one tests, if only to assess the effectiveness of the teaching method and the result it has achieved. Evaluation of creative achievement and response is fraught with problems. Measures to try to assess creative abilities in physical education are in the process of development but as yet are very inexact and exploratory (Foster, 1971a). Although the attempts have been largely unproductive they could be given a further element of validity with more research refinement. In another study concerned with evaluation in modern educational dance, Mottershead (1972) replicated research originally carried out at Anstey College of Physical Education. The same problems of criteria were met in these studies, and results remained highly speculative, and only indicative of trends. Evaluation is often at the core of disagreement about the value of educational gymnastics and the solution to this problem is remote. A psychometric approach will probably not be either successful or acceptable. The curriculum development movement, with its emphasis on definition of aims and objectives, learning experiences, and subsequent evaluation of these offers a growth area which is more acceptable to the various interested parties in the debate.

Many of the criticisms are accepted in general terms by movement-orientated practitioners and planned approaches are being advocated more than formerly. There is value in more detailed planning and identification of what may be termed as 'learning-outcomes'. Teachers are confused by the terms 'free', 'expressive', and 'educational' in gymnastics. This confusion often leads to pure play on the apparatus instead of imaginative progression. This is the case especially where teachers have misunderstood the concepts of what is understood by the term 'progressive education'. If this is interpreted as a 'laissez-faire' approach, then the point is valid. If 'planned-intervention' on the part of the teacher characterizes the work, then the criticism is less tenable.

A recent international conference of the Physical Education Association of Great Britain and Ireland was concerned with the place of educational gymnastics in education. At this conference, all the same old ground was again covered. One was constantly hearing the comment, 'But we've surely been here before.' Most of the papers read made heavy weather of the same semantic problems repeatedly mentioned in this work and used as examples the work of children which might have been a carbon copy of similar work seen two decades earlier. Only one contribution, by Bet. Mauldon, broke completely new ground by asking the question, 'What is educational about gymnastics in any form?' This paper severely questioned most of the basic assumptions which have been made for years about gymnastics in education. The thesis was not accepted uncritically but at least badly needed new thought was stimulated on this rather hackneyed topic.

Work based on Laban's principles is said to neglect 'the habitual, functional use of the human body'. In this view, there is no guarantee that the body's mechanisms are not being abused, however well-intentioned the teacher or the system. A related case is that, 'the mental activity in Basic Movement may predominate over free and vigorous effort, leaving the body tense and strained at the end of a lesson.' Here there is a danger of forgetting about the body while the mind is cared for. These views are typical of individual reactions and comment which abound in movement. The subject generates intensely individual response. One can draw from almost every article and paper, and pick up the pros and cons of arguments dealing with the elements of the subject rather than its overall method.

There has been general criticism in education concerned with the highly verbal element of most classroom learning. Amidon (See Amidon & Hough, 1967) has evolved his two-thirds rule for classrooms. He says that in classrooms two-thirds of the time, someone is talking; two-thirds of the talk is teacher-talk; and two-thirds of that talk is direct telling. Johnson (1972) examined this proposition in physical education lessons and concluded that the two-thirds rule could become the nine-tenths rule in physical education lessons. Naturally, this method does not show the non-verbal response taking place through physical activity, but it highlights the high verbal content of the teacher's contribution in dance and educational gymnastics. It raises the question, 'Is there too much direct telling; is there perhaps too much 'teaching' and not enough open-ended suggestion?' However, in this inquiry, physical education teachers used more praise than 'classroom' teachers; and dance lessons included more content than educational gymnastics classes. No formal conclusions are drawn from this work but the results are cautionary and invite examination of the role of the teacher using verbal instruction and direct telling in her lessons.

Counter argument

The case against Laban has built up over the years. Then counter argument has been advanced in defence of approaches based on his work. Examples of this were given earlier. Lack of research has also brought a counter-attack. Rainey (1967) showed that non-verbal learning, far from being a luxury, was a necessity. He defended the lack of formally conducted research by an argument which was based on the assumption that when scientific method stops, discoveries go beyond this by the artistic approach. Empirical psychometrics do not constitute a royal-road to success. Brewster Ghiselin in *The Creative Process* showed that many of the world's greatest thinkers worked without formal research backing, and that many of their discoveries were made intuitively at first and had to wait for scientific verification until much later. Arthur Koestler (1964) in *The Act of Creation* presents a similar case. Much of the creative process and production which he describes is based on pure intuition. The description of how it arose is also provided from introspection rather than any carefully controlled inquiry. Russell (1958) follows a similar line to Rainey and comments that, 'In the twentieth century, Rudolph Laban formulated his philosophy through the same empirical approach (observing) and eventually developed a method of observing and recording movement which has enabled us to gain increasing insight into the importance of movement as an expression of inner impulses reflecting temperament and mood.' She believes that empiricism is not enough in itself, and that the creative insights of the perceptive artists often give insights into problems that could not be produced by empiricism alone.

Current American view shows the lack of experimentation, and paradoxically that this has led to other insights being reached by different methods. These views are summarized in the statement:

> Because of the way it pulsates at the inner core of our lives, it seems intuitively right to assume that aesthetic experience plays an important role in psychological health. For centuries, man has known that an aesthetic experience embodies a therapeutic component, but to date, there have been almost no scientific efforts to isolate this component experimentally.

At the same time that empiricism is not all, it does demonstrate other truths and identifies new research areas.

Psychology provides many examples of breakthroughs in knowledge which have come about through 'less than scientific' techniques. Many of these are now enshrined in academic respectability. The theories of intelligence assessment have their origins in very poorly validated experimental procedures initially. Piaget's early work is very suspect if one uses criteria concerned with his research design. The whole field of measurement of creative abilities can be castigated in the same way as Laban's ideas at this point in time. Laban's work is probably what Cattell called, 'blind empiricism' rather than 'blind theory' (Warburton, 1969). Cattell supports the former against the latter in the phrase, 'To pursue theories which you cannot verify (or refute) is to chase uncatchable geese.' He regards it as a compliment to be told that, 'you have no pre-experimental theory.' This probably marks out a creative field of endeavour. It is true of Laban's work. There is support for Laban's approaches:

> Despite its limitations, a descriptive taxonomy (and Laban's principles could be considered to be this) has the advantage of being close to real-life and hence practicable.

Watertight, theoretical models are stimulating intellectually but are of little use in the classroom. The sequence for Laban's work, in these terms, may be:

  i blind empiricism
 ii development of models
iii eduction of theory

The first part is operative. A start is made on the second and opportunities can open up for the third aspect.

A rapprochement

A severe dichotomy exists between the pro- and anti-Laban factions; and yet while this is so, there are strands which bring them together. There is a danger that blind following of Laban's ideas leads to children not 'approaching' creative heights, but settling for an inadequate destination. Neither is the goal one of merely 'approaching'. It should contain an element of 'achieving' as well. It is the latter point which is sometimes stressed by the anti-Laban argument. The extreme fringe of both camps present entrenched positions offering little scope for productive development. It is when there are moves at the centre that a rapprochement seems likely and a common-sense approach which takes something from both sides emerges as a workable solution. Steel (1951) over twenty years ago showed weaknesses in both arguments:

> The old . . . had a preconceived curriculum founded on presumed scientific concepts of physiology and anatomy. The new . . . is weak in established knowledge of subject-matter and curriculum; its main criteria being that the individual should be interested and stimulated by it.

He concluded:

> Our final analysis of the difference between the old and the new suggests that in some aspects, they should be considered as complementary rather than opposed.

A rapprochement indeed. Such a view, if seen now in the light of curriculum changes and the current trends in education, must look at physical education in schools as an integrated model covering all known and documented elements of the subject. Such a subject would be at the heart and not on the periphery of school learning experiences.

Often, controversies have revolved around teaching styles and claims have been made that direct teaching was associated with one ideology, while inferential teaching styles were associated with another. Wherever good teaching has been observed, it has usually involved an amalgam of styles. Teachers from Laban or opposing backgrounds cannot be successful with a single teaching style. The best teaching in this subject takes in an amalgam of teaching styles; moves easily from exposition to inference, and from formal didacticism to arranging for discovery to take place.

The last word draws a parallel between the work of Bruner and Laban. With regard to Bruner:

> American educators have welcomed Bruner's directives so unreservedly that his influence has come to carry something verging on political weight. There is the danger then that the very revolution that has received so much of its impetus from Bruner's hand will stall for lack of optimum confluence.

The same argument applies to Laban. The profession must achieve 'optimum confluence' by compromise, or the subject will lose further status and esteem.

Higher Education

Introduction

The main impact of Laban's work has been in primary and secondary education. Increasingly, his influence is extending to higher education as the patterns in this sector are changing, and approaches and content are becoming more diffuse.

The principal areas of interest are concerned with the changing role of higher education in our society today, the development of movement studies as a course option in some institutions of higher education, the teaching of movement notation, and the links between the universities and these changing concepts of physical education. Other subjects include the study of crystallography, movement therapy, movement and science, research, and evaluation procedures. Therapy, notation and examinations need further study as particular facets of higher education.

The place of physical education and its component parts in higher education is very much linked with the status of the subject and its academic respectability. Except in very minor areas, the subject has been treated in higher education as physical recreation and its position has been outside the mainstream of academic work until recently. This is true both of the art of movement, and physical education in the more traditional sense. Physical educationists have been concerned about this and the literature contains many examples of attempts to change the position and to prove the rightfulness of the subject as a study comparable with others at this level.

Typical of the arguments is that of Meredith (1968) who states:

> If the Art of Movement is to scale the ladder of scholastic respectability and convince the world of its importance in the conventional academic examination-ridden atmosphere of the

contemporary curriculum, it must do it the hard way, not by preaching unspecified spiritual values but by demonstrating its contribution to culture.

The implied criticism of some advocates of the art of movement, that they preach spiritual values, is the same criticism made earlier, and labelled ingenuous and naive. It indicates a lack of concern for the intellectual stringency which the subject can offer, and a failure to evaluate the content of the discipline in a rigorous, academic manner. This is not the fault of Laban or his ideas which provide opportunities for the depth of study suggested. It is fairly and squarely the responsibility of those influential educationists who have applied his work to education and who have been in a position to guide the lines of its development. Justifications of the subject's tenability have been in cosmic, rather than artistic terms. Laban's mystical mode of apprehension has hypnotized the educationists more than the actual content of his thoughts; the justifications have sometimes stressed the affective to the exclusion of the cognitive values.

A recent influential article (Evans, 1972) dwells on the crisis nature of the present:

> The James report has clearly brought the subject to a cross-roads and selection of the routes it has to follow will decide its future place, role and status within education.

Two important guidelines are indicated. First, the significance of movement in education is stressed, and second, the importance of recreational aspects of the subject are noted. These guidelines emphasize the relevance of movement and changing concepts of recreation in higher education. It is the movement sector which is the particular concern of this study. The plea is for some kind of movement study in higher education. The subject must be viewed as a curriculum subject and an integral part of the educational process. Can movement studies be included as an academic discipline and if so, is there a Laban influence to be seen in the suggested content of the subject?

Movement studies
The case for dividing the study of human movement from

physical education has been discussed. Most commentators have put their own interpretation and particular slant on the division but the broad schism is fairly constant. One of the growth points of this trend was an article in *The Leaflet* by Brooke (1967). This drew attention to the diversity of physical education specialisims and showed the need for a common descriptive terminology (the semantic problem once more). It proposed the bases for a taxonomy of human movement and is important for this study because the classification does acknowledge the work of Laban and the particular influence it has had on modern educational dance and educational gymnastics. The difficulties of direct application of Laban's principles to pre-determined skill patterns, as in a javelin throw or a forehand drive were shown; yet it acknowledged that the four defined realms of Time, Force, Space and Flow were very pertinent to any movement performed, and that they form the verbalized structure for both the student and the pupil. It is this theme – its fundamental position with respect to any movement performed – which suggests a change of emphasis for Laban's work. The early suggestion for a taxonomy has been developed by Webb (1972). She put much of the work into perspective and established a case to try to show that:

> . . . the theoretical content of physical education is not irrelevant in the study of the subject whether at school or at post-graduate level . . . and to ask if movement studies may be accepted as the discipline of physical education.

In delineating the theoretical content of physical education, Webb identified a wealth of study and research areas, and presented a statement of the codified body of knowledge, which could provide the core of the discipline of human movement studies. She argued a case for the establishment of theoretical courses of study of movement at both secondary and higher education levels. She realized that this is a young and developing subject but saw development taking place and counselled:

> Every science begins as philosophy and ends as art, it arises in hypothesis and flows into achievement.

The case presented by Webb is formidable. She shows that the theoretical content exists and argues its relevance to life today.

The views she expresses are typical of a newer generation of physical educationists. This school is well-versed in Laban's work, but not so close to the man as his original interpreters. They are prepared to question many assumptions made for his work, and use it in a more flexible, contributory manner as part of a wider concept of movement studies. They are concerned to de-systematize the work, and to develop it, particularly as a course of study in higher education. This heralds a new chapter in the Laban story. After an innovative start and an adventurous spurt in schools, there has been some stagnation and a consolidation of effort. Laban's ideas have been attenuated. This may have been an essential part of the development pattern. It has persisted too long and the new growth of thinking, which owes little to the man, but more to his work, is overdue. It comes at a particularly opportune time now as the reconstruction of higher education is beginning. Reviewing physical education and the James report, Hewitt (1971) emphasizes the need to find:

> some intellectual leverage, as opposed to physical and technical clout,

for the subject. He does not see the subject being intellectualized but its nature being analysed. He assumes a place for physical education in higher education. His article draws attention to a new concept for physical education in higher education. It will be necessary now to provide courses for students who wish to study the subject but who are not committed to teaching. The content of these courses is the really important element which is supplied by Webb's proposed taxonomy. Not all will be relevant but with pertinent selection, much will be. It is certain that some of Laban's work will be included and in making the overall choices, Laban's influence will have been exercised.

At Lady Mabel College, the faculty of human movement studies has developed a range of courses based on how movement develops in the growing child and also other courses studying sports science, where the emphasis is on an examination of motor impairment, sports injuries and their causes, the physiology of exercise, and the formation of training schedules and fitness profiles. Other courses are concerned with the aesthetics of movement where the emphasis is on a study of aesthetic evaluation and appraisal which stresses an artistic rather than a measurement approach. This aesthetic study is concerned with a detailed examination of appropriate theoretical concepts in dance, drama and music. The fourth area of study centres on communication and its links with human movement. Here the emphasis is on social interaction and the role of movement in communication. A series of courses like this obviously draws on a variety of influences but it can be seen that the areas of study are genuinely related to many elements of the Laban work already identified in this book.

The work quoted is recent but as long ago as 1958, Bodmer, a geneticist, was presenting a scientific approach to the study of movement. He showed how a scientific approach begins with observation and description. Relationships are noted which initiate a formal analysis to describe the relationship in abstract terms. New relationships come out of this and are translated back to reality and investigated to discover their meaning. This is a perfect description of how movement can be studied in higher education. It draws on discovery learning, links practice and theory, and is rooted in empiricisim. Bodmer concludes:

> In this light, I consider Laban's work as laying the foundations of such a scientific study of human movement.

It is ironic that this article was written in 1958. Its predictive value is now seen to be high. The relationship with higher education is also there, as Bodmer postulated the use of Laban's theories at higher educational levels as one means of opening up further creative development lower down the educational system, in a perceptive article, full of germination points which failed to produce any recognizable impact. We must assume that physical educationists were not ready for these moves at that time. There is more evidence that they are willing to follow this course now.

A similar position exists in Scotland. The functions of specialist physical education colleges are seen solely in terms of the professional preparation of teachers. They have added nothing to the body of knowledge underlying the subject. This is also true of England up to about 1970. Since then, the work on movement studies as outlined, and the growth of the research already mentioned have redressed this balance. The appointment of research officers in colleges is one way of helping to validate courses of movement studies in higher education. The field is virgin at present and the need for early and effective evaluation of new courses is evident. There may be other ways to accomplish this. The value of setting up research in physical education colleges is that there ought to be immediate feedback to the students who are the future teachers of movement studies in institutions of higher education.

Notation

Several forms of notating movement have been invented. The well-known codes are Labanotation and the Benesh system. Laban's first system of notation was called, 'Kinetographie'. Like many other of his projects, Laban did not develop the idea fully and it was mainly left to Albrecht Knust, Ann Hutchinson and Valerie Preston-Dunlop to formalize the system. Labanotation is the American name for the development of Laban's early work. It is a set of pictorial symbols that can record simply and accurately any movement of the human body. There are two kinds of notation symbols. The one commonly known as 'Labanotation' records the time, duration and the shape pattern of the movement. The other, 'effort notation', records the expressive factors of movement. Together, these two sets of symbols can give a detailed account of any movement.

The claims of notation to be included in courses of higher education have been made consistently over the years. In America, notation appears in most dance major programmes. In England, it is included as a component in all BEd syllabuses of the study of human movement. Valerie Preston-Dunlop opened the Beechmont Movement Studio with courses in notation as a prime interest. These flourished for a while and students from colleges of education and other institutions of higher education, and the universities, went for short courses. The studio is now closed. During the time it operated, Valerie Preston-Dunlop and her assistant, Paddy Macmaster developed 'Motif Writing', a simple system, drawing on Laban's work, to record motion ideas or purposes behind actions. This system has been used in schools and colleges with some success. A reasonable proficiency can be obtained quite quickly using this method. Its use has considerable support – 'The technique of motif-writing has added a new dimension in the use of notation. It has enormous potential and is, I think, the greatest single advance in the contemporary field of creative movement study. It is a source of enrichment adding new impetus to progress in all aspects of movement education' (Rosewarne-Jenkins, 1966/8). There are those who are critical of it and doubt its extreme usefulness, but generally it is seen as a possible tool for use in movement study at a higher education level. Its use is also advocated for work in the related arts, particularly drama.

The use to be made of notation is all-important when considering its place in higher education. If it is thought of as a tool for research, or as an aid to understanding movement principles, it can be considered. If it is merely a training ground for teachers to teach it to others, little justification can be found. If the view that, 'At present, the only occupation for a student of Labanotation is as a teacher of Labanotation' is true, the case for inclusion is weak. If it can be shown that the technique assists study in a variety of ways and makes scientific observation more possible, the case is much stronger. At present, there is little future for it in schools judged against these criteria but courses now being offered in colleges and universities may be extended, particularly to include students from associated disciplines such as Organization and Method, and Management Consultancy.

Universities and Polytechnics

A study programme financed by the Winston Churchill Memorial Trust, has surveyed the place of physical education in the universities. In 1970, when this study was completed the general position was that most universities had appointed a Director of Physical Recreation. Most courses offered were recreative and voluntary. Some universities offered courses in physical education to their post-graduate certificate students preparing for a teaching career. The work at Birmingham, which offers physical education at under-graduate level as one subject in a Combined Subjects degree, is picked out for special mention. The growth of post-graduate studies for higher degrees at many universities is noted. Doctoral level work is described as 'slow so far'. There has been general expansion in all the fields noted since 1970, but the survey indicated the position accurately at that time.

As long ago as March 1963, the Journal of Physical Education ran a series of articles advocating physical education as a field of study in the universities but these articles produced little which could be used in support of such a move.

The BEd degree has brought a variety of movement studies into the university orbit via the colleges of education, and the subject is now generally accepted as an element in this degree. Human movement as a means of communication, human movement studies, dance, movement are all option titles accepted for BEd in the particular sphere which includes Laban's contribution. The influence of Laban's work across a wide spectrum of activities is seen when BEd Syllabuses are scrutinized. The progress of BEd over the next decade is significant. The development of the subject at university level is dependent to some extent on the success of BEd and similar courses.

North (1971) tries to account for the lack of university-level work and forecasts its development:

> The study of human movement in Western culture is probably in its infancy, and its full development lies in the future. No doubt, some years hence, there will be a department of movement in every university, and it will be recognised that the scope of the subject is as broad as that of any other discipline at present studied.

North sees movement study applied to the arts, including architecture, modelling and painting, maladjustment, therapy, education, industry and commerce. This pattern is developing slightly. Physical educationists have advised the mechanics department of a university on movement study problems recently. The Manchester School of Business Studies has used movement consultants to indicate the importance of a knowledge of posture, gesture, facial-set and movement-groupings in business dealings. Exploratory talks have taken place in one college of education to assess the possibility of taking their work within the university. If this happened, they would be in a position to draw greatly from university expertise and strengthen the Department of Physical Recreation with plant and professional knowledge. It is from such mergers as these that course development could ensue.

The fact the several colleges of education are moving into new polytechnic organizations raises the possibility that movement studies will receive a fillip in higher education. The trend is that where this is happening, the old physical education department of the college is receiving considerable strengthening and academic stiffening from existing, related polytechnic departments.

This brief is not formally concerned with American practice but a parallel seems admissible if it elucidates a position in England. Development in education in England has often followed American trends. At present, many American universities have dance major programmes whose scope is extending to include higher degree possibilities. If these trends are followed, and there is an indication that some of them may be if the current concepts of liberal arts colleges are developed, then the American patterns may provide appropriate models for our courses.

In summary, the search for academic respectability which has been referred to many times is at the heart of the matter. Sympathy for the inclusion of movement studies as a course exists in many universities. When the codified body of knowledge which constitutes the discipline is tightly identified, it is likely that course options will develop in widely different forms, initially under the auspices of a variety of university faculties.

Little documented study exists about movement education in the polytechnics. The most fruitful sources of information are the prospectuses of the various institutions. These show a pattern not dissimilar to the university development. The polytechnics are supporting courses for industry, at the request of particular firms, which draw on movement observation skills. Also, some of the units forming part of a polytechnic structure, whose roots are in the technical college system, are still offering 'pre-diploma type' courses which are open to students who wish to take a course of study prior to attending a college of education, or the polytechnic's own faculty of educational studies.

An example of the type of short courses mounted by polytechnics is provided by the Polytechnic of Central London. In September 1972, they organized a three day symposium on

'New directions in recreation'. The emphasis on this course was on recreation in the widest sense and the appeal was to managers, directors, planners, teachers, lecturers and students. The focus is unmistakably physical education. The course covered all the main contemporary areas of the subject. The polytechnics expansionist policy suggests that they will look favourably on any emergent disciplines where courses can be developed. One college of physical education has recently become an integrated part of the local polytechnic. Other colleges are considering the possibility of a similar move to create the situation already referred to. Such mergers will enhance the possibility of movement studies courses in polytechnics.

Evaluation

Evaluation presents the same difficult problems in higher education as elsewhere. The need is for the development of flexible, imaginative evaluation procedures. They do not exist at present but must be developed before the subject can make headway at the tertiary stage. The criterion problem is the uppermost reason for the lack of empirical research, followed by the shortage of research workers, apathy among present physical educationists, and a failure to identify the main problems in detail. Evaluation must be tackled by the profession at this level above all others. Movement Studies will make little headway in higher education unless an acceptable level of reliability and validity can be built into evaluation techniques. Evaluation can be reconciled with creative response, and need not lead to inflexibility. The plea that since movement is an art form, it need not be quantified is unacceptable. This view cannot prevail if movement studies is to be taken fully into the sphere of higher education.

There is no evidence in the work of Laban that he eschewed evaluation. The principles he developed are themselves evaluative instruments. They provide the basis for assessment of the qualitative aspect of movement and also quantify elements in the movement. It is a mark of the systematization of his work that has taken place when for years there has been an outcry against evaluation procedures. The anti-measurement lobby is powerful and influential. It invokes a case which rests on the view that measurement is anathema to creative response, and that an affective experience needs no quantification. Pure measurement in psychometric terms can be attacked. However, it should not be dismissed completely. Skills acquisition, motor-performance, carefully-defined physical activities can all be measured in acceptable terms, and this research must be developed and extended. Evaluation in total is something much wider in concept than psychometric testing. It includes any form of grading, assessment, reaching standards, and marking. It subsumes objective and subjective elements and is implicit in all forms of teacher-interaction with the learning process. In the passage used to summarize an earlier section, Armytage put evaluation firmly as an integral part of curriculum construction. It must be included in planning, but its ethos must be all-embracing and its practical application flexible.

To continue with Laban's own view of evaluation, he gave implicit details of how to evaluate objectively using observation techniques (Laban 1957). His title, *The objective observation of subjective movement and action* indicates clearly that he is talking about the very root of what has become a major schism; and yet in this article, he is advocating evaluation. In an article published posthumously, he looks into the future of movement study and shows that:

> It is not beyond the bounds of possibility that the line of development of the language of movement as well as the ideas expressed in this language will lead to the scientific dance of a scientific epoch.

In this article, he envisages the academic study of his work at a later date, and also foresees that scientific study brings analysis and evaluation to bear on what had been a synthesis on his part.

Evaluation and research are complementary and it is an important trend that the latter is developing. The form of development is important. There is a wide variety of research underway, most of which involves the use of non-parametric techniques which permit a greater flexibility in assessment procedures. This is right for a subject like movement where stereotyped forms of testing are patently unsuitable to the media. This research is illustrated in recent Year-Books published by Chelsea College of Physical Education, and occasional papers from Carnegie and Anstey Colleges. At other specialist physical education colleges research in connection with the BEd degree is indicative of a national trend of involving students in carefully-controlled inquiries which use a variety of evaluation procedures.

The work of Webb on taxonomies, already examined, implies evaluation. In order to progress to the construction of models and the development of theories, evaluation of the hypotheses implicit in the taxonomical classifications is essential.

Some physical educationists are putting the case for evaluation but are against objective or psychometric evaluation. They quote the work of Jenkinson (1969) at the Ontario Institute for Educational Studies who says:

> We have abundant evidence that teacher observation that is systematic, structured, recorded immediately and undertaken at specific intervals affords data which is frequently more valid and have greater predictive value than standardised tests or external examinations.

Most supporters of evaluation agree with this view. It supports the real need for flexible systems, imaginative approaches and new-thinking on evaluative procedures. If the Laban influence affects evaluation at all, it will be to support the use of systematically controlled observation, set against clearly defined criteria which may be established from his principles.

It could be that evaluation exercises in movement studies will benefit from such techniques as video-tape, advanced photographic techniques and the various interaction schedules now being developed in the field of non-verbal communication. At Lady Mabel College, all these approaches are used as an integral part of new courses involved with movement studies, most of which owe at least something to the work of Laban.

Crystallography

Laban was fascinated by the structure of crystals and read cosmic significance into their formation. He used them in allegorical forms to explain his metaphysical ideas and drew heavily on crystal forms to explain basic human movement patterns. He wrote extensively on the subject and suggested the science of crystallography as worthy of further consideration in the movement context which his work opened up (Laban, 1951). This work has been heavily criticized, and sometimes dismissed out of hand especially by the philosophers. There is, however, support for Laban's approach to the study of crystal forms. He used the science in a novel, unique way when he applied it to Movement. 'Recent work on the X-ray of microscopic shadows, virus crystal shapes and patterns, seem familiar to us from our work in the space-harmony, of course it should! Laban did not discover the ico- or any of the other crystal forms, symbolic patterns and shapes, or rhythms. These have been known and used and passed down through generations from ancient times. But he did see their relationship in a new way, in a way very related to movement, and was able to bring what, to our knowledge, is a fresh approach to the study of man and his universe' (North, 1964a/b).

Laban suggested further study of crystal forms. Is there any place for the science of crystallography in education? In movement studies, there may be! As a general form of study, however, it has little future as Laban envisaged it.

Much of Laban's work with crystals was metaphysical and echoes the work of Froebel. In *The Education of man*, Froebel makes most of the points which Laban uses in his own writings on the study of crystals many years later. However, it is when Laban begins to apply the crystallographic ideas to movement that he becomes more credible. With the advent of 'new maths', three dimensional shapes have been included much more in mathematical studies. Laban's use of the icosahedron to identify certain areas in space around the body which are specially stressed, has mathematical implications which have not been researched at all. In modern terms, Laban could be regarded more as a 'creative mathematician' than a 'mystic metaphysic' if one concentrates on the functional aspect of his use of crystals and ignores the allegorical use and speculative chemistry.

In short, crystallography presents a research area of movement studies. It opens up fields of inquiry too lightly dismissed by some critics because they looked at the mysticism more than the practical application to movement. As a post-graduate research field, it still offers possibilities for imaginative inquiry.

Therapy

It has been shown earlier that Movement therapy has been used in the treatment of psychotics, physically disabled, in cases of brain damage and in maladjustment. If this use of movement is appropriate, the therapists must be specifically trained. The colleges of education, who provide more movement-trained students than any other sector, at present do little specifically concerned with the therapeutic uses of movement. Movement therapy provides a possible growth point in the application of movement studies to particular vocational fields. Little exists at present. It is a contemporary issue and an area of development for the future.

Leisure

As automation increases and technological change makes established careers obsolete, educationists have become more concerned with 'Education for leisure'. As part of a blueprint for education in the future, Gould (1968) contributed to the symposium an article entitled, *Looking ahead in Education*. He outlined fundamental changes which have taken place in our society and showed that education and leisure will become almost synonymous in the future for many citizens. A study of the writings of Galbraith, Macluhan and the predictive social commentators reveals similar expected patterns. Baroness Burton (1967) establishes the same line, linking automation and leisure to show the challenge which it presents to physical education.

Physical education will increase its scope in schools to embrace the many-faceted leisure activities which are emerging as new life-styles develop in the Seventies. As this happens, the work of Laban may be conceived in a dual role. His influence will still be felt in the field of modern educational dance but this is likely to remain a feminine activity. His provision of a classification which may lead to a movement theory can be used in some way by all branches of any new and widened concept of physical education. The men in physical education have no objection to using Laban's analysis in any way to help both functional and expressive movement throughout their work. It is any attempt to push them into a dance-orientated curriculum which is resisted. As new leisure activities are included in the curriculum, coaching of these, in the hands of fully trained movement practitioners, will draw on movement principles. The fastest growing sport in the country today is squash. This sport provides a perfect example of how a player's performance can be improved by an analysis of his movements, and a fuller understanding, by the player, of the tensions and stresses his body undergoes as he moves to anticipate shots. Revisions to the curriculum, such as the inclusion of leisure activities and sedentary society complementary activities (health gyms, exercise machines) may enhance Laban's influence rather than diminish it. Laban has influenced curriculum change in the past and if current trends continue, he may do so, in a new way, in the future.

Physical education in the future will become more concerned with catering for new life-styles. Increasing sedentary ways of life mean that publicity focuses on the care of the body and contrived exercise as a way of life. Activities which are stressed should bring pleasure and social contact. The accent is moving to therapeutic exercise rather than sport. The indications that this is a correct forecast are already present. Health clubs formed with profit as the main aim are already here, indicating a lack of provision in the social services. Obesity is a problem and has given rise to clubs specializing in weight-reduction through exercises. 'Keep-fit' booms in further education and voluntary bodies. Yoga is now popular and LEA's are providing classes in this activity. Sauna baths and health clubs are to be found in every small town and even disc-jockeys are able to promote exercises to assist house-bound women. An analysis of all these activities shows that they promote movement which draws heavily on Laban, and of course others associated with his work, particularly Dalcroze. The development of Laban's influence is now spreading. It is still concerned with education but as the aims of education change and school-based learning gives way to wider views of education, so the influences on education change their emphasis.

A survey by Owen (1969) has shown that dance is listed as the biggest single interest by a large sample of adolescent girls.

The development of more individual, expressive modes of dance owes something to the Laban influence which today's teenagers have experienced in schools. At discotheque level, the movement principles have become very stylized, rigid and conforming, but in professional interpretations, Laban ideas are used to extend popular dancing into another pop-art form. This new-art form is rejected by some Labanists. Would Laban himself have rejected it? His concern with the pop-art and various schools of art-nouveau of his day indicate that his attitude may have been more accepting than some of his disciples.

As the leisure boom develops, Laban's influence, until now mainly centred in the institutions will tend to affect less formal elements of movement. If this enriches the quality of life and the movement conscience of the masses, this is to be welcomed and would have delighted Laban.

Research

The need for more research has been reported throughout this inquiry. If it is done, it will be undertaken in an institution of higher education. The research function must be a feature of any movement studies faculty.

Little research has been undertaken to study movement and development. How does movement interact with growth and development? What are appropriate movement experiences for each stage of development? What is the relationship between particular movement experiences and emotional and social development? Similarly, there have only been embryonic studies concerned with the relationships of movement to personality. The data we have concerning posture and gesture is mostly intuitive. Little structural work has been attempted, and yet the links between posture and gesture, and self-concepts are the basis of many proposed hypotheses.

There is a lack of research in movement which emanates from other disciplines. Physical scientists and physiologists throw productive light on the science of movement as only tentatively identified by movement-orientated researchers. Similarly, the work of Waldron on minimal brain dysfunction formerly centred at the Department of Audiology at Manchester University provides interesting links between movement and cerebral activity.

Numerous claims have been made for dance, none of which are supported by objective evidence because Laban's propositions are not verified by formal research. Many of these are wild and completely unsubstantiated.

> . . . modern dance . . . has now taken its rightful place . . . bringing with it a wealth of material to the service of the creative facility. (Collins 1969).

> . . . while collaborating, he learns to show forbearance, forgiveness and appreciation of those round him. (Collins 1969).

> . . . dance . . . is an unconscious form of outlet and exercise introducing them to the world of the flow of movement, and strengthening their spontaneous faculties of expression. (Laban 1948).

> . . . it is as a contribution to the aesthetic and creative aspects of education that dance has a place. (Russell 1965).

The view that much is claimed 'on trust' for dance must be accepted. In twenty-five years of Laban Art of Movement no research whatever has got beyond the fringe. The greatest need in professional training in physical education, as in all subjects, is for professional judgements based on research evidence rather than amateur opinions based on feeling and intuition. There is a reluctance on the part of movement educationists to submit what they are doing to evaluation on the grounds that it is difficult, and that quantification is not the sole criterion of the value of an activity. This view may be a disservice to themselves and the subject. Just as there is little research evidence to support the subject, there is no evidence to say that it would fall down when examined under experimental conditions. It has many points in its favour when subjected to philosophical analysis, literary and analytical study, and in dialogue and debate. Why should it not be equally well supported in a psychometric or similar inquiry? No research ever whitewashes a subject. Pros and cons are stated, and hypotheses sometimes rejected. This does not, however, invalidate the subject. It is essential that evaluative research is undertaken to test carefully-posed hypotheses.

These topics have emerged from this study as suitable for research. Their examination ought to aid understanding of difficult areas and provide predictive data which can be used as the basis for subsequent curriculum development:

Space-harmony.

The personal life of Laban.

The role of movement in the adaptation of man to his environment.

The nature and purpose of movement in education.

Movement therapy.

Kinetography and its place in schools.

Human movement studies and physical education in the leisure-age.

The place of a theoretical study of human movement in schools.

The training of physical education aides, auxiliaries and coaches.

Examinations

During the last few years, the question of whether to gear courses in physical education to an examination syllabus in GCE and CSE has been raised repeatedly. Although the question has reached a focal point during the last few years, as long ago as 1961, an article in the *Times Educational Supplement* (6.1.1961) advocated a GCE course in modern educational dance. This article made a plea for financial help to begin work on an examination syllabus and also made the point that:

> By leaving the subject outside the scope of GCE, the subject itself is penalised.

This issue divides the profession completely. Some believe that an examination system would act as a strait-jacket on the work; others believe that this is the way to academic respectability, a proper allocation of timetable time, and a more meaningful share of the curriculum.

The pro-examination case points out that the place and status of physical education is a universal problem and quotes support from two articles in the *Times Educational Supplement* (31.10.69). This case favours GCE 'O' and 'A' level courses in movement studies and differentiates between movement studies and physical education, viewing the latter as the applied branch of the former.

A cautionary note (See Bambra, 1971) shows concern about the aims and objectives of physical education and differentiates two aspects of the role of the physical educationist:

> Whether we regard ourselves primarily as educators using the medium of physical activity to promote physical, mental and socio-emotional growth, or whether we see ourselves as subject specialists concerned to bring children to a high level of skill and understanding in a variety of physical activities.

According to which view is taken, the answer to the question of examining in the subject can be varied. This report concludes:

> We can subscribe to the establishment of examinations in physical education only if we can prove to our own complete satisfaction that our educational aims will be better achieved by the aid of such an examination.

There is a case for the formal examination of some of the work which is undertaken under the omnibus title, 'physical education'. The use of the term movement studies to designate elements of theoretical study is now widely accepted, as is the split of this area from the applied aspect of the work. Laban's ideas have provided a systematic body of knowledge which is capable of interpretation and further development. It is suitable material for evaluation and could provide an element of a syllabus which would properly culminate in an examination.

Examinations should not be thought of in terms of three-hour written papers. Many other forms of examination suggest themselves, namely: continuous assessment, practical work, prepared topics, empirical studies, use of observation schedules, examinations using 'seen' questions, the use of notes under otherwise examination conditions, and viva arrangements. In any of those arrangements in physical education or human movement studies, the work of Laban would undoubtedly figure. In an interpretive subject, where aesthetics and creative response are paramount, many of these examination arrangements are appropriate. It is possible by these means, to sample a student's knowledge of theoretical rationales, to use these in practical work, and to present personal interpretations of them. The fear that evaluation will mean the rôte-learning of facts is unfounded and is not a prerequisite of testing procedures. The suggestions made have more flexibility, and allow far more width of evaluating approach than the formal use of the ubiquitous rules-tests so often seen as part of courses in physical education.

Examinations in movement studies will not be totally associated with Laban's work. The work of other movement practitioners needs to be included to present an overall pattern of thinking and development in the subject. Laban's work is part of the movement spectrum. It has influenced a system which is culminating in the need for evaluation through a suitable form of examination. Laban did not provide 'the system' itself, but a contributory element of it, and in this view, his work is accepted by all sections of the profession. The initial work in the examination sphere already undertaken by several CSE Examining Boards, and especially that stemming from a Mode Three arrangement supports this view, and also offers an adventurous starting point for other work.

Other issues
Most of the contemporary issues concerning physical education in higher education are compounded. They draw from each other for support and justification, and equally are used to refute counter-argument and disprove points. The philosophical issues which are splitting the profession are fundamental to the practical issues which they presume. If the philosophical points are clarified, many of the practical problems can be resolved pragmatically even if they cannot be solved. A gulf exists between the teachers, and the theoreticians and teacher-educators. Much of the debate is solely the concern of the last two groups, and takes place in the sector of higher education. Teachers in schools rarely figure in the reported debates or in decision-making at any level beyond internal school matters. This must alter if the ideas promulgated are to be transformed into reality in schools. The maxim of the educational administrator, 'From advice to action' needs to be followed. Action can only occur if specific attempts are made to involve teachers in the evaluation of innovation. The teachers also need support in carrying out curriculum innovation in schools which can often be supplied

by both the human and physical resources which are available in higher education.

The relationship of Laban's work to contemporary problems is as complex as the problems themselves. The impact which his thinking has made in education has acted like an echo-sounding device in all dialogue. The new approaches coming from his work, the analysis of movement he made possible, and the extension of his influence beyond dance, has meant that his influence has permeated into every sector. Sometimes it has been prescriptive, often predictive, and occasionally divisive. It has been prescriptive in the way it has laid down a framework for the study of movement in many different areas. The predictive influence is in the emerging centrality of the movement idea in new patterns of curriculum organization. It has been divisive in the examination and evaluation debates. In total, the contribution has been broadly positive. Where it has been hotly contended, the ultimate influence may be positive in the long-term if, out of the debate, solutions emerge which are appropriate to contemporary needs. Nowhere is there evidence of a completely negative influence in higher education or elsewhere.

APPENDIX ONE

Principal correspondence received from Oscar Bienz

1.

20th October, 1972

Dear Mr Foster,

Your enquiry into Brother Rudolph von Laban, Laban de Laban. Count Laban's activity in the Swiss Masonic Lodges, was sent to me, over various Lodges for reply. I was continually associated with the Laban School and the Freemason's Lodges to which Laban belonged during his three years stay in Switzerland. When I was a member of that school, I advised him sincerely, as he had a great position and progressive mind.

Laban came in 1916 to Zurich, and started a eurhythmic and personality cult, which had great success, due to excellent propaganda, and the absence of any other Ballet School. I was the first scholar. His teaching was based on Count Keyserling's idea, the development of an individualistic personality. His assistant was Mary Wigman, who founded later her own school with great success.

In 1917 during a congress of vegetarians, he went with his school to Monte Veritas above Ascona. There, he came in contact with Theodor Reuss, who was the only claimant and Grandmaster of the OTO 99 degrees Scotch, Memphis and - Rites - Order Templar Ritual. Reuss was initiated in 1910 in Lodge 238 in London.

To enable Reuss to start his own Lodge and make use of his patents, he initiated Laban into all the 99 degrees of this order in a couple of days. The Labanists were prepared for admission and the Lodge 'Verita Mystico' was opened. In the autumn, Laban returned to Zurich, and with new-found brethren, a new lodge was founded, 'Libertes et Fraternitas' which still exists today. The working was originally co-masonic with esoteric teaching, but consequently, the sisters, which were all Labanists, were dropped, and the lodge worked then in the Scottish Constitution. In 1924, the Swiss Grand Lodge accepted admission and the National English Constitution Teaching was now used.

Trouble now or even before 1919 started in the Lodge on account of the speedy raising of Laban into the higher degrees, and a book written by von Brunsdorf Bergen was openly thrown on the market but did little to shake the Lodge or Laban. Laban was advised to go to Germany apparently on account of his numerous alliances with women. He left leaving a lot of debts, 60,000 Swiss francs to the Worshipful Master and 5,000 from me and many others I know of which were never repaid.

Laban was never a truly initiated Freemason. He later switched over to a Jewish Lodge in Berlin where he was acting as Ballet Instructor at the Opera House. In my opinion, he was a shadow Cagliostro. All our records in the 'Libertes et Fraternitas' from 1907–1920 were destroyed by anxious brethren who feared a German invasion of Switzerland which never realized.

I know that the above information doesn't give you much hope to place Laban's three year connection in Switzerland in a favourable light. It may however be that he started it again in his last years in England in a more realistic and true manner. (He did not J.F.).

All my connections with Laban ceased in 1920. Unfortunately our correspondence got lost through the death of my father and mother.

I am the only living member of that period but for me, Masonry has been my life.

I hold myself at your disposal should further information be required.

Sincerely and fraternally yours,
OSCAR BIENZ

2.   23rd November, 1972

Dear Mr. Foster,

In answer to your letter of 26th October.

Count Cagliostro, an Italian, was a wizard and a pseudo-mason. The history of free-masonry has some lines on him, specially his Paris sojourn.

I am sending you the original of the Laban photograph (used on the jacket J.F.).

Regarding Carl Reuss, he wrote a book titled *Ascona* which was published in 1964. (This book is quoted in the text J.F.).

Quasi-masonry at this time was like co-masonry. Something like the Theosophists in England with Annie Besant as Grand master. In 'Libertes et Fraternitas', more conservative Swiss joined and after three months, due to some Jewish brethren's immoral behaviour with these ladies, real masonic science was prevented.

Count Herman Keyserling from the School of Wisdom in Darmstadt influenced Laban. His teachings were concerned with the spiritual essence, mostly for wisdom in Asia, with emphasis on immortality, and of course, Austrian literature, mostly classics.

Laban's interests outside dance centred around Max Reinhardt, Stefen Zweig and his Jewish friends.

He had no philosophical training but he studied Mystic, mainly Gurdjieff, Ouspensky, Herman Hesse, etc.

Laban's main personality characteristic was his height - over six feet - of which he made plenty of use and movement in dancing demonstrations.

Some important dancers, I recall, like Perrotet from the Dalcroze Institute in Geneva, Mary Wigman, and Schuber assisted in building up his five fundamental dancing steps.

At the time I knew him, Laban lived with a Mlle Lederer near Zurich. He was not at all involved in politics.

As a teacher he was reasonable and friendly.

You ask about his family, marriages and mistresses. He co-habited with almost all the not-so-young dancers, which were mostly Jewish. He told me that his father was War Minister at the Austrian court under Emperor Joseph.

Laban came from Darmstadt to Zurich in 1916 and he was then just starting out to realise his ambition, as he couldn't do it in Germany. In this he was helped generously with money from the Lodge Brethren, and from some of his German friends then in Switzerland. He also told me he was previously in Paris.

I believe that is the essence of which I can remember Laban.

Fraternally yours,
OSCAR BIENZ

P.S. After 1920, I switched over to engineering and am now an engineer. The stage lights were not for me and I had no admiration for the Germans.

APPENDIX TWO

Other Studies of the Work of Laban With Particular Significance for this Inquiry

There are three particular studies which have examined the work of Laban which merit special mention. These are the work of Curl (1967a), Thornton (1971) and Redfern (1973).

Curl carried out a critical study of Laban's theory and practice of movement. He showed that these had been the instruments of revolutionary change in teaching method. This study used the critical analysis of the philosopher to examine Laban's work and was highly discerning. The conclusion was that 'Laban's 'art of Movement', 'gymnastics' and 'effort' theory defy analysis; they are mythical in conception and their claims are grossly exaggerated.' Curl recommended that Laban's mystic metaphysics be made over to meet the demands of a sound psychology and aesthetic theory. His study is referred to as specific points are discussed. Here it remains to comment on the work generally, and show how it differs significantly from this inquiry.

To take the latter point first, Curl's study was undertaken as a philosophical exercise, and was mainly concerned with Laban's theory and practice of movement. He devoted only one chapter to Laban as an educator and pedagogic theorist, and so was not particularly concerned with this brief.

It is comparatively easy to destroy the basis of a theory (if such it be) which has been presented by a man working in a language which he learned fundamentally after his sixtieth birthday. Laban, like Piaget, suffered from his translators, and found difficulty in expressing ideas concerning kinaesthetics in a verbal medium. His work is open to attack and vulnerable if one queries terminology and the meaning of words. Curl attacks the base of Laban's theory with some success but the edifice of his achievements in education has been built separately and its validity does not now rest entirely on the merits of the base structure. Curl says that:

such mystical and esoteric theory must be eliminated from the syllabuses of any serious academic study.

This is not acceptable. Laban provided a taxonomy and a first model rather than a theory. What is needed now is a rigorous examination of the areas which he opened up and for which he provided a framework. This has not been done. For instance there has been no book on space-harmony published in England since *Choreutics* by Laban appeared posthumously in 1966. *Choreutics* is the result of exploratory inquiry and is not a definitive work. It presupposes further intensive study and is a perfect example of 'Laban the initiator'. The book demands further development but it has not been forthcoming. The development may come from those with intense practical experience and knowledge and a high academic attainment, perhaps in mathematics. Few, however, enter into the study of human movement with these qualifications.

Curl misses the point with his strictures on Laban, and his recommendation of exclusion of work based on his less-than-perfect systems. Laban should not be accepted as the provider of an inflexible set of rules so much as the presenter of basic designs which have possibilities for imaginative development built into them.

Curl has raised many pertinent issues. His impact on this study has been to provide a focus of informed, carefully presented opinion which is used to weigh evidence to the contrary.

Thornton's book derives from a dissertation presented at Leeds University. The original study examined the impact of Laban's work on physical education in England and Wales, with special reference to the indoor lesson. This was a minor study and formed the basis of his book published in 1971. The book is a useful overview of Laban's work. It is descriptive and partisan in that there is an uncritical acceptance of almost everything said and done by devotees of Laban's work. He states blandly, 'From his principal works, from his conversations with friends and his lectures, there emerges an implied philosophy of education.' This is the manifestation of the problem noted by Curl, and exactly the kind of false assumption which has been made about Laban's work. This approach has held back the development of human movement studies and helped to give the subject a low status in the academic hierarchy.

The term 'Education' is viewed very widely by Thornton. In his chapter on 'Principles of Education', he includes mastery of movement on the stage, and choreutics, a technical study of the moving body in space. His study differs from this inquiry on this count. In this book Education is defined in terms of experiences deriving from formal schooling in the educational system of England and Wales.

Thornton makes little attempt to relate Laban's ideas to what actually goes on in schools. In a few sentences of what Curl termed, 'mixed-metaphysics', he stumbles through a jumble of meaningless expressions like, 'the child's effort-life', 'acquisition of action and effort habits by dancing', 'total immersion in the flow of movement', and 'the covert and overt behaviour of man'. His twenty-four references in this chapter are all taken from Laban himself, and offered as support for his theme. This does not suggest a balanced, unbiased view.

A therapeutic role for the teacher is implied when he says:

> It is the task of the properly trained teacher to find those dance movements which offer the possibility of balancing discordant attitudes and of promoting a healthy growth of personality.

Even in specialist colleges of physical education, the student-teacher is not trained at all for the role implied here.

It is when Thornton moves into the empirical field that his work becomes entirely suspect and incredulous. He used questionnaire techniques in an attempt to chart the influence of Laban on education. In mounting his inquiry, he employed none of the accepted research principles (Oppenheim, 1966) usually associated with these techniques. However, he concludes naively:

> It was not intended that the results obtained *would be statistically significant* (sic) nor will they be interpreted in a way which suggests that the findings are conclusive for the whole country.

After which he asserts:

> The trends indicated . . . can be regarded as inevitable and entirely logical.

Later he refers to his questionnaire results as 'concrete facts' and treats them as such.

In his conclusions, Thornton is guilty of the most sweeping generalizations and makes assumptions of appalling magnitude. He says:

> Yet these attributes (man's intellect and knowledge) have, *in the last fifty years* fragmented, isolated and destroyed the unity of his life.

> His classification of movement has focused attention upon its important constituents and can give man the opportunity and the means to view his own life in its true perspective.

Thornton's work highlights a type of approach all too common in the study of Movement. It is important to mention this study specifically here to account for the decision to look again at some of the issues allegedly covered by Thornton.

The work of Redfern (1965, 1973) is an important contribution about the nature of human movement studies and interpretations which have been put on Laban's work. She makes 'a preliminary attempt' to examine the problems of meaning in Laban's theories, attempts some re-interpretation and studies the claims for the inclusion of dance in the curriculum. She expects counter arguments and ongoing debate, and fundamental to her thesis is that whatever 'movement' may mean, it must mean not remaining in the same position!

Redfern uses her philosophical expertise and practical experience to question many assumptions made about Laban's ideas. She shows the need for development from the positions stated by Laban and is critical of those who have used his writings as a blueprint to follow slavishly.

A List of the Published Works of Rudolph Laban prior to 1938

Die Welt des Tanzers. Stuttgart: Walter Weifert, 1920.

Festwille und Festkullur in *Die Tat*, Heft 11, 1922.

Methodik zur Tanzschrift und tanzerische Tanze. 2 Hefte 1925–1930.

Des Kindes Gymnastik und Tanz. Oldenburg Stalling, 1926.

Gymnastik und Tanz fur Erwachsene. Oldenburg Stalling, 1926.

Choreographie. Jena: Eugen Diederichs, 1926.

Schrifftanz, Methodik und Orthographie. 1928.

Tanztheater und Bewegungschor. In Gentges J. *Tanz und Reigen*. 1928.

Deutsche Tanzfestspiele. Dresden. 1934.

Ein Leben fur den Tanz. Dresden: Carl Reisner, 1935.

Die tanzerische Situation unserer Zeit. Essays by Laban and others 1936.

Note:

This list has been compiled with the help of Mr G. F. Curl and Professor J. M. Ritchie. It is probably not complete but represents those works located at this time.

REFERENCES

AMIDON E. & HOUGH J. B. (Eds.). *Interaction Analysis: Theory, Research and Application.* Reading, Massachusetts: Addison-Wesley. 1967.

ARMYTAGE W. H. G. Education and Physical Education. Conference Report, Education and Physical Education – Complementary Studies. G. F. Curl (Ed.) Pub. by Dartford College of Education. 1972.

ARNOLD P. J. *Education, Physical Education and Personality Development.* London: Heinemann, 1968.

ASIMOV I. *Biographical Encyclopaedia of Science and Technology.* London: G. Allen & Unwin, 1966.

BAMBRA A. J. Examinations in Physical Education. Eastbourne: Chelsea College of Physical Education Year Book, 1970/71.

BANTOCK G. H. Towards a theory of popular education. *Times Educational Supplement,* 12 and 19th March 1971. (Also reprinted – See R. Hooper 1971).

BIENZ O. In a letter to the author. See appendix one for text, 1972.

BODMER S. Polarity. *Laban Art of Movement Guild Magazine,* 1960, 25, 18-22.

BODMER W. E. A scientific approach to the study of movement. *Laban Art of Movement Guild Magazine,* 1958, 21, 39-40.

BONHAM-CARTER V. *Dartington Hall. The History of an experiment.* London: Phoenix House, 1958.

BRAITHWAITE M. *Medau Rhythmic Movement.* London: Medau Society G.B. and N.I., 1955.

BRITTON E. L. The struggle for recognition. *British Journal of Physical Education.* 1972, 3, 34-5.

BROOKE J. D. A taxonomy for human movement. *The Leaflet.* London: Physical Education Association. Aug/Sept., 1967.

BROWN M. C. & SOMMER B. K. *Movement Education: its evolution and a modern approach.* Reading, Massachusetts: Addison-Wesley, 1969.

BROWNE P. Teaching dance-drama. *British Journal of Physical Education.* 1970, 1, 66-7.

BRUCE V. Dance and dance drama in Education. Unpublished M Ed Thesis. University of Leicester, 1962.

BRUCE V. Dance and Dance Drama in Secondary Modern Girls'

Schools. *Laban Art of Movement Guild Magazine,* 1963, 30, 42-6.

BRUCE V. *Dance and dance drama in Education.* Oxford: Pergamon, 1965.

BURTON B. The challenge of leisure. *Physical Education,* 1967, 57, 25-8.

CHARLES C. M. *Educational Psychology.* The instructional endeavour. St. Louis: Mosby Co., 1972.

CHENEY G. & STRADER J. *Modern Dance.* Boston, Massachusetts: Allyn and Bacon, 1971.

CHESTERS G. E. The relation of expressive work to the needs of children. *Journal of Physical Education,* 1950, 42, 125.

CILENTO D. Tarot: All on the cards. 1972, *Vogue,* 8, 129.

CLARKE E. & W. The development of Physical Education. In symposium; see Armytage W. H. G. (1972).

CLEGG A. B. Is Physical Education an art or a science? *The Physical Education Year Book,* 1964/5. London: Physical Education Association.

COLLINS C. *Practical modern educational dance.* London: Macdonald & Evans, 1969.

CORLETT H. Modern Educational Gymnastics today. *British Journal of Physical Education,* 1970, 1, 63-6.

CORTLETT H. & WEBB I. M. Movement Theory - a justification. *Physical Education Year-Book* 1971/2. London: Physical Educational Association, 1971.

CRAUS R. *History of the dance in art and Education.* Englewood Cliffs, New Jersey: Prentice-Hall 1969.

CURL G. F. A critical study of Rudolph von Laban's theory and practice of movement. Unpublished M Ed. Thesis. University of Leicester, 1967a.

CURL G. F. Philosophical Foundations II. *Laban Art of Movement Guild Magazine,* 1967b, 38, 7-17.

CURL G. F. Philosophical Foundations IV. *Laban Art of Movement Guild Magazine,* 1968, 40, 27-38.

CURL G. F. Philosophical Foundations VI. *Laban Art of Movement Guild Magazine.* 1969, 43, 37-44.

DALCROZE J. One (1921) of several reprints of a book attributed in English to M. E. Sadler. See M. E. Sadler (1912).

DE MILLE A. *The Book of the Dance.* London: Hamlyn, 1963.

DENNIS W. Causes of retardation among institutional children. *Journal of Genetic Psychology,* 1960, 96, 47-59.

DEWEY R. M. The significance of Rudolph Laban's studies in human movement. *Laban Art of Movement Guild Magazine,* 1961, 26, 11-24.

DUNN M. Movement as an aid to the understanding and development of personality. In *Movement, Dance and Drama.* Conference Report, University of Hull, March 1970.

DUTOIT C. L. *Music, Movement, Therapy.* London: Dalcroze Society, 1970.

ELMHIRST L. In a letter to the author, 1972.

EVANS J. C. The way ahead. *British Journal of Physical Education,* 1972, 3, 33–4.

FERDINAND P. A letter to the editor, *British Journal of Physical Education,* 1970, 1, 125.

FOSTER J. *Creativity and the Teacher.* London: Macmillan Education, 1971.

FOSTER J. *Discovery Learning in the Primary School.* London: Routledge & Kegan Paul, 1972a.

FOSTER J. The balance of studies for students of physical education. In symposium see Armytage W. H. G. (1972) for publication details. 1972b.

FOSTER R. The analysis of movement. *Laban Art of Movement Guild Magazine.* 1960, 25, 23–9.

FULLER L. *Fifteen years of a dancer's life.* London: Herbert Jenkins, 1913.

GARRISON K. C., KINGSTON A. J. & McDONALD A. S. *Educational Psychology.* New York: Appleton-Century-Crofts, 1964.

GAUMER D. The art of movement in Education. *Laban Art of Movement Guild Magazine,* 1960, 24, 32–42.

GHISELIN B. (Ed.) *The Creative Process:* A symposium. New York: Mentor, 1955.

GILLIOM B. C. *Basic Movement Education for children:* Rationale and teaching units. Reading, Massachusetts: Addison-Wesley, 1971.

GOULD R. Looking ahead in education. In P. Bender (Ed.). *Looking forward to the seventies.* London: Colin Smythe, 1968.

GRUNDEN C. The uncomfortable relation of physical education and human movement. *British Journal of Physical Education,* 1972, 3, 6–7.

GURDJIEFF G. I. *All and Everything:* an objectively impartial criticism of the life of man, or Beelzebub's tales to his grandson. London: Routledge & Kegan Paul, 1967.

GURDJIEFF G. I. *Meetings with remarkable men.* London: Routledge & Kegan Paul, 1963.

HAHN K. *Kurt Hahn: a life span in education and politics.* London: Routledge & Kegan Paul, 1970.

HALL F. *An anatomy of ballet.* London: Andrew Melrose, 1953.

HALPRIN A. The process is the purpose: an interview with Vera

Maletic. *Dance Scope,* 1967/68, 4, 11-18.

HARRISON J. A. Private Schools in Doncaster in the nineteenth century. Unpublished dissertation submitted for the ACE Institute of Education, University of Sheffield 1957.

HAWKINS A. M. Dance as a discipline. In Smith N. W. (Ed.) (1967).

HENDRY L. B. A study of certain aspects of the Physical Education profession. *British Journal of Physical Education.* 1972. 3, 5-7.

HEWETT S. Physical Education in a multi-purpose college. *British Journal of Physical Education.* 1971, 2, 19-20.

HOGGART R. Only Connect. The Reith Lectures. *The Listener* 18th Nov. 1971, Vol. 86. No. 2225.

HOOPER R. *The curriculum:* context, design and development. London: Oliver & Boyd, 1971.

HORST L. *Pre-classic Dance Forms.* New York: Dance Horizons re-published 1968 (first published 1937).

HOWLETT R. G. A list of theses concerned with the art of movement. *Laban Art of Movement Guild Magazine*, 1969.

HUTCHINSON A. The use of Labanotation in Schools. *Physical Education* 1956, 48, 40-3.

HUXLEY A. *The Devils of Loudon.* London: Chatto and Windus, 1961.

JAMES J. M. *Education and Physical Education.* London: Bell. 1967.

JAMES J. M. A letter to the editor. *British Journal of Physical Education.* 1971, 2, 33-4.

JENKINSON I. Work quoted by E. Biggs and J. R. Maclean, *Freedom to Learn.* Reading, Mass: Addison-Wesley, 1969.

JOHNSON S. A study of the differences between the verbal interaction in Mathematics lessons and that in Physical Education lessons using the Flanders' category system of interaction analysis. Dissertation in part-fulfillment of BEd. requirements. Rotherham, Lady Mabel College 1972.

JOHNSTONE M. A. *The physical training of girls.* London: Sidgwick and Jackson, 1924.

JORDAN D. *The dance as education.* London: Oxford University Press, 1938.

JORDAN D. *Childhood and Movement.* Oxford: Blackwell, 1966.

JORDAN D. Education and Dance. Talk given at Woolley Hall, 18.3.72, to the West Riding Movement Study Group and cir-culated privately by them.

KENNEDY D. What is Dance? *Journal of Physical Education.* 1950, 42, 2-8.

KIRSTEIN L. *Dance. A short history of classic theatrical dancing.* New York: Dance Horizons republication (3rd Edition), 1969.

KOESTLER A. *The Art of Creation.* London, Hutchinson, 1964.

KÖHLER W. *Gestalt Psychology*. New York: Liveright. 1929.

LABAN R. *Der Narranspeigal*. Published originally in Germany in 1920. Translated by L. Auberbach and printed in the *Laban Art of Movement* Magazine, 1955, 15, 12-16.

LABAN R. *Ein Leben fur den Tanz*. Dresden. 1935. Published in England in 1975 by Macdonald and Evans under the title 'A life for dance'. Translated and annotated by Lisa Ullmann.

LABAN R. President's Address to the Annual General Meeting. *Laban Art of Movement Guild Magazine*, 1947, 1, 1-3.

LABAN R. *Modern Educational Dance*. London: Macdonald and Evans, 1948.

LABAN R. What has led you to study Movement? Answered by Rudolph Laban. Report in *Laban Art of Movement Guild Magazine* 1951, 7, 8-11.

LABAN R. The Laban Lecture. A reported account in the *Laban Art of Movement Guild Magazine*, 1954a, 12, 22-4.

LABAN R. The work of the Art of Movement Studio. *Journal of Physical Education*, 1954b, 46, 23-30.

LABAN R. A series of articles in the *Laban Art of Movement Guild Magazine*. Dec. 1954c, celebrating Laban's birthday.

LABAN R. The objective observation of subjective movement and action. *Laban Art of Movement Guild Magazine* 1957, 19, 2-13.

LABAN R. Movement concerns the whole man. *Laban Art of Movement Guild Magazine* 1958, 21, 9-12.

LABAN R. Light/Darkness. Posthumous publication of an earlier writing. *Laban Art of Movement Guild Magazine*. 1960, 25, 13-17.

LABAN R. The Laban Lecture. Reprint of a 1939 speech. Reported in *Laban Art of Movement Guild Magazine*, 1961, 26, 11-24.

LABAN R. *Choreutics*. London: MacDonald and Evans, 1966.

LABAN R. and LAWRENCE F. C. *Effort*. London: MacDonald and Evans. 1947.

LAMB W. On being a movement artist. *Laban Art of Movement Guild Magazine*. 1964, 32, 33-6.

LAMB W. *Posture and Gesture*. London: Duckworth, 1965.

LANGE R. Philosophical foundations and Laban's theory of Movement. *Laban Art of Movement Guild Magazine*, 1969, 43, 9-16.

LANGE R. The nature of dance. *Laban Art of Movement Guild Magazine*. 1970, 44, 6-22.

LANGER S. K. *Feeling and Form*. London: Routledge & Kegan Paul. 1953.

LAYSON J. Review of 'Isadora Duncan - the Russian years' by I. I. Schneider. *Laban Art of Movement Guild Magazine*. 1969, 42, 25-7.

LESTER SUSAN *Ballet here and now.* London: Dennis Dobson. 1961.

LEWIS J. G. The professional preparation of teachers of physical education. Unpublished M Ed. Thesis University of Leicester. 1967.

LONDON COUNTY COUNCIL *Movement Education for infants.* Published by London County Council, 1963.

LYNEHAM D. *The chevalier Noverre - Father of modern ballet.* London: Sylvan Press, 1950.

MACKINNON D. W. Personality Correlates of Creativity. A paper presented at the second conference on thinking. (NEA Washington DC 2-4 May 1963 - Mimeo).

MAJOR E. Physical Education during the past century. The first fifty years - 1900/1950. *Physical Education Year Book* 1969/'70. London: Physical Education Association.

MARTIN J. *The Dance.* New York: Tudor Publishing Company, 1946.

MASLOW A. H. *Towards a psychology of being.* New York: Van Nostrand, 1968.

MAULDON E. Two articles concerned with Oskar Schlemmer and his relationship to Laban. See *Laban Art of Movement Guild Magazines:* 1974, 53, 5-20; and 1975, 54, 7-18.

MAYEROVA M. Le balet est mort, vive le balet: *Laban Art of Movement Guild Magazine.* 1957, 18, 28-9.

MEIER W. The influence of Rudolph Laban's work on the development of the Keep Fit Association of England and Wales. *Laban Art of Movement Guild Magazine.* 1966, 36, 30-3.

MEREDITH G. P. Reporting an article in the Chelsea College of Physical Education Year Book, Vol. 1, 1968/9.

MOORE L. *Artists of the dance.* New York: Dance Horizons, 1968.

MOORE S. *The Laban Art of Movement Guild. In the Laban Art of Movement* Guild Magazine. 1971, 46, 26-32.

MOORE P. R. & WILLIAMS E. A study of Movement in football. *The Leaflet.* London: Physical Education Association, July 1967.

MORISON R. *A Movement Approach to Educational Gymnastics.* London: Dent, 1969.

MORLEY J. Music, dance and speech - a unity. *Laban Art of Movement Guild Magazine,* 1972, 48, 4-9.

MORRIS M. *My life in Movement.* London: Peter Owen. 1969.

MOTTERSHEAD L. A study of the assessment of creative work in Modern Educational Dance. Study presented at Lady Mabel College of Education (4th year B Ed. Course). 1972.

MUNROW A. D. *Pure and Applied Gymnastics.* London: Arnold, 1955.

MUNROW A. D. *Physical Education. A Discussion of principles.* London: Bell & Sons, 1972.

MURRAY R. L. *Designs for dance.* Washington, DC: Dance division of

REFERENCES 177

American Association for Health. Physical Education and Recreation, 1968.

NORTH M. Laban Lecture. Reported in *Laban Art of Movement Guild Magazine,* 1964a, 32, 12-19.

NORTH M. Symbolism. *Laban Art of Movement Guild Magazine,* May 1964b, Included in same article as M. North (1964a).

NORTH M. *An introduction to movement study and teaching.* London: Macdonald & Evans, 1971.

NOVERRE C. E. (Ed.) *The life and works of the chevalier Noverre.* London: Jarrold & Son, 1882.

OPPENHEIM A. N. *Questionnaire design and attitude measurement.* London: Heinemann, 1966.

ORFF C. Orff - Schulwerk: Past and Future. Music in Education, Sept/Oct. 1964. A production of a speech by Prof. C. Orff at the opening of the Orff Institute in Salzburg, 25th October 1963. (Translated by Margaret Murray).

OWEN J. W. *Studies in Physical Education.* Physical Education Association of Great Britain and N. Ireland, 1965.

OWEN J. W. Some observations on physical activity and leisure. *Physical Education,* 1969, 61, 13-16.

PERCIVAL S. W. Physical Education for what? Its role in the secondary school. *Physical Education* 1967, 39, 176.

PHENIX P. H. *Realms of meaning.* New York: McGraw Hill, 1964.

PIAGET J. *The Science of Education and the Psychology of the child.* Translated by D. Coltman. London: Longmans, 1971.

PRESTON-DUNLOP V. *A handboook for modern educational dance.* London: Macdonald and Evans, 1966.

PRESTON-DUNLOP V. The Beechmont Movement Study Centre. *The Leaflet.* London: Physical Education Association, May 1967a.

PRESTON-DUNLOP V. Laban's analysis of movement. *Physical Education,* 1967b, 59, 49-53.

RAINEY H. P. Non-verbal learning: a luxury or a necessity. (See Smith N. W. (Ed.) (1967)).

RANDALL M. The movement approach - a need for clarification. *Physical Education.* 1956, 48, 15-17.

RANDALL M. *Modern Ideas on Physical Education,* London: Bell, 1967.

READ H. *Education through Art.* London: Faber and Gaber, 1943.

REDFERN H. B. *Introducing Laban Art of Movement,* London: Macdonald & Evans, 1965.

REDFERN H. B. *Concepts in Modern Educational Dance.* London: Henry Kimpton, 1973.

REID L. A. Movement and meaning. *Laban Art of Movement Guild Magazine.* 1970, 45, 32-42.

RICHARDS C. M. Trends in the curriculum of the primary school. *Journal of Curriculum Studies*, 1972, 4, 3–10.

RICHARDSON E. *The environment of learning. Conflict and Understanding in the Secondary School.* London: Nelson, 1967.

RICHTER H. *Dada. Art and Anti-Art.* London: Thames & Hudson, 1965.

RIESS C. *Ascona* published in Switzerland in 1964.

ROBERTS C. Movement Training for Girls. *Journal of Physical Education*, 1953, 45, 93–6.

ROSEWARNE JENKINS M. A. Creative movement writing. *Physical Education* 1966, 58, 41–3.

ROSEWARNE JENKINS M. A. The contribution of modern physical education to the arts through dance and drama. *Physical Education Year Book 1968/69.* London: Physical Education Association.

ROSS A. K. and POSTMA J. W. The rhythmical gymnastics of Dr R. Bode. *British Journal of Physical Education.* 1954, 46, 56–65.

ROWLAND K. *The shapes we need. Notes for teachers. Looking and Seeing.* Part 3. London: Ginn 1965.

RUNES D. D. *A pictorial history of philosophy.* New York: Philosophical Library, 1959.

RUSSELL J. Movement – a comprehensive education. *Laban Art of Movement Guild Magazine* 1957, 18, 14–19. Also published in the *Times Educational Supplement* 4.1.57.

RUSSELL J. *Modern Dance in Education.* London: Macdonald and Evans, 1958.

RUSSELL J. M. Modern Educational Dance in the secondary school. *Physical Education,* 1961, 53, 81–5.

RUSSELL J. M. The place of modern educational dance in the curriculum. *Physical Education Year Book* 1963/4. London: Physical Education Association.

RUSSELL J. *Creative Dance in the primary school.* London: Macdonald & Evans, 1965.

RUSSELL J. *Creative Dance in the secondary school.* London: Macdonald & Evans, 1969.

SADLER M. E. *The eurhythmics of Jaques-Dalcroze.* London: Constable & Co, 1912.

SATTERLEY D.J. and BRIMER M. A. Cognitive styles and school learning. *British Journal of Educational Psychology.* 1971, 41, 294–303.

SEVERS J. A planned approach to educational gymnastics. *The Leaflet,* London: Physical Education Association July 1969.

SHAWN T. *Dance we must.* London: Dennis Dobson, 1946.

SHAWN T. *Every little movement.* New York: Dance Horizons, 1963.

SIMPSON H. M. Physical Education and the Arts. *Physical Education.* 1967, 59, 54–60.

SMITH N. W. (Ed.) *Focus on Dance IV.* American Association for Health, Physical Education and Recreation, 1967.

STACK P. *Movement is Life.* London: Collins Harvill Press, 1973.

STEEL W. L. The 'old' and the 'new' in Physical Education. *Journal of Physical Education.* 1951, 43, 42–5.

STEPHENSON G. Freedom in acting or the latest cliché. *Laban Art of Movement Guild Magazine.* 1960, 24, 29–31.

STEWART W. A. C. *The Educational Innovators Vol. II. Progressive Schools 1881–1967.* London, Macmillan, 1968.

STORR A. *The dynamics of creation.* London: Secker and Warburg, 1972.

STRAND MAGAZINE. An unsigned article about Loie Fuller. *Strand Magazine.* Newnes, Jan-July 1894, 7.

STREICHER M. *Re-shaping physical education.* Edited by B. E. Strutt. Manchester University Press, 1970.

SWEENEY R. T. *Selected readings in movement education.* Reading, Massachusetts: Addison-Wesley, 1970.

TANNER J. M. and INHELDER B. *Discussions in Child Development.* Vols. 1–4. London: Tavistock, 1953–6.

TAYLOR I. A transactional approach to creativity. *Journal of Creative Behaviour.* 1971, 5, 190–8.

THORNTON S. *A movement perspective of Rudolph Laban.* London: Macdonald & Evans, 1971.

TIMES EDUCATIONAL SUPPLEMENT. Movement Education. Attributed to a correspondent. *Times Educational Supplement* 6.1.61., p. 10.

TORRANCE E. P. *Guiding Creative Talent.* Englewood Cliffs, New Jersey: Prentice Hall, 1962.

TORRANCE E. P. and TORRANCE P. Combining creative problem-solving with creative expression activities in the education of disadvantaged young people. *Journal of Creative Behaviour,* 1972, 6, 1–10.

ULLMANN L. Movement Education. *Laban Art of Movement Guild Magazine.* 1960, 24, 19–28.

ULLMAN L. Writing in the *Laban Art of Movement Guild Magazine,* 1964, 32, 20–6.

ULLMANN L. Presidential Address 1967. *Laban Art of Movement Guild Magazine.* 1967, 38, 54–6.

VERKAUF W. *Dada. Monograph of a movement.* London: Alec Tiranti, 1957.

WARBURTON F. W. The assessment of personality traits. In J. F. Morris and E. A. Lunzer (Eds.). *Contexts of Education – Development in Learning.* London: Staples Press, 1969.

WARD M. K. Report of a talk given by Mr (Now Sir Alec) Clegg. *Laban Art of Movement Guild Magazine.* 1951. 7. un-numbered.

WEBB I. M. Physical Education – Its aims and objectives. Eastbourne: *Chelsea College of Physical Education Year Book 1970/1.*

WEBB I. M. *The theoretical content of physical education.* See Armytage W. H. G. 1972 for source.

WEBSTER C. M. Physical Education today and tomorrow. *Physical Education Year Book 1969/70.* London: Physical Education Association.

WEINER J. & LIDSTONE J. *Creative Movement for Children.* New York: Van Nostrand, Reinhold Co, 1969.

WERTHEIMER M. *Productive Thinking.* London: Tavistock, 1961.

WHITING W. A. Retrospect and a point of view. *Physical Education.* 1956, 48, 35–9.

WILLETT J. *Expressionism.* World University Library. London: Weidenfeld and Nicolson, 1970.

WILLIAMS L. C. Physical training or physical education. *Physical Education* 1966, 58, 178, Nov.

WILLIAMS L. C. Art and Science of Movement. *British Journal of Physical Education* 1970, 1, 58–62.

WILLIAMS T. I. (Ed). *A biographical dictionary of scientists.* London: A. & C. Black, 1969.

WOLFF C. *Psychology of gesture.* Translated from the French by Anne Tennant. London: Methuen, 1945.

WOOTEN B. J. O. Roots of the American Modern Dance. *Laban Art of Movement Guild Magazine* 1957, 19, 21–4.

INDEX

INDEX

DATE DUE

MAY 1 7 1984			

HIGHSMITH 45-220